The Good Feeling

about

What A Feeling!

'Reading What a Feeling! is like opening the curtains and finally shedding light on all the habits and beliefs that keep us from having our best relationships. Filled with practical strategies and real, heartfelt stories (and wonderful, often hilarious sidebar comments from Toni), Toni helps us realize that having better relationships is a learnable skill, one that's never too late to learn.'
Michelle Gielan, bestselling author of *Broadcasting Happiness*

'This is a wise, warm and 'whole-hearted' book from a 'whole-hearted' woman and is offered as a gift to our often broken world. Toni honestly and candidly shares her insights into the nuances of human behaviour. Toni explores powerful, important questions and provides really helpful insights that when practised will support the development of meaningful and sustainable relationships.'
Justin Robinson, Director; Positive Education Institute, Geelong Grammar School

'Toni's way of unpacking neuroscience and making it available to everyone in humorous, revelatory and practical ways will have your relationships humming! She's a whizz at making sense of the pitfalls that can terminate or damage our relationships.'
Petrea King, Founder, Quest For Life & Author of *Up Until Now*

'Toni's book, What a Feeling! is smartly, frequently laugh-out loud, funny, candid and full of heart. A must-read combination of real life stories and practical strategies to find happiness within all of your relationships, including the one with yourself."
Shawn Achor, New York Times bestselling author of *The Happiness Advantage* and *Before Happiness*

'This is the book I've been waiting for! It's the perfect blend of science and memoir, from someone who turned a loveless marriage into a 40 year love affair. Toni's wisdom—and her explanation of relevant psychology and neuroscience—is both fun and easy to put into practice.'
Christine Carter, PhD, author of *The Sweet Spot* and *Raising Happiness*

'What a Feeling! is equal parts captivating storytelling and science-based insight. Toni's ability to dance between story and science makes this book so readable and so relevant. Toni's honesty, rawness and lived experience leaves no room for fluff. In a field littered with academics and anecdotes, it's rare to read a book which cuts through the noise in such a powerful and practical way. I couldn't put it down.'
David Bott, Author *Teach Positive*

'Toni Powell's newest book, What a Feeling! is an approachable and entertaining read that answers and validates many of our burning relationship questions.'
Jennifer Moss Cofounder, Plasticity Labs , Author of *Unlocking Happiness at Work*

'Toni is a "giver" and she has enriched my life and I believe is responsible for enriching the lives of all who come in contact with this graceful powerhouse. Her surprising book will continue that enrichment.'
Tony Barry, Actor and Activist.

'This book is the best book ever written. Really. And I usually don't give compliments.
Evelyn Vogt, Wise Person

OKay, and yes, I do admit she is also my mother.

What a Feeling!

What a Feeling!

Finding love, *freedom* and the good life through creating great relationships

Toni Powell

What a Feeling!

Author: Toni Powell

Cover design: Patrick Walsh, Toni Powell

Editing: Mary-Lou Stephens, Mark Nebauer, Evelyn Vogt

www.tonipowell.me

ISBN 978 0 9942960 4 7

for

Philip Powell

I love you a million Jonathans

Also by

Toni Powell

THE YELLOW CAR

How I stopped driving myself crazy

Available at all good bookstores,
Amazon & from the author

www.tonipowell.me

CONTENTS

*'Not life,
but good life,
is to be chiefly
valued.'*

SOCRATES

1

CHASING THE GOOD LIFE

When my husband, Phil, first proposed to me, we were both 19. My answer was blunt, one that didn't give him hope of a future happy union.

'Oh, fuck off. Don't be ridiculous.' Yeah, I have issues.

Pretty much everyone we knew agreed with me, a marriage between a couple like us was ridiculous. Nevertheless, as you'll read in the next chapter, we went ahead and tied the knot. This knot has, despite all predictions to the contrary, endured, happily entwined, for 40 years.

Did it turn out that we were a perfect couple after all? Not remotely. What did happen was we developed an enduring interest in relationships that was sparked, initially, by the question 'How can we create a good marriage?'

This fascination with relationships served us well when, in more recent years, two major relationship breakdowns, each in their own way, blew our worlds apart.

BUT FIRST THE GOOD NEWS STORY

In November 2006, ABC's Australian Story ran an unusually cheerful and warmhearted episode called *'Let There Be Light'*. It was the account of how a community came together to stage an event and the unlikely tale behind it. It was a story about Phil and me and our wonderful, impossible, huge and beautiful dream.

I think I was in shock for a month.

The almost miraculous international success of a short film we'd made with family and friends had introduced Phil and I to the world of film festivals. When I say miraculous, I mean that none of our crew were filmmakers. We were as surprised as anyone.

I'd always had an interest in film and after our experiences attending film festivals, I came up with a big vision. This was during the early days of YouTube and I was already worried about internet content and disturbed by a lot of what I saw on television. I could see the internet would do a good deal of parenting for our coming generations and this scared me. Our idea was to throw hope, laughter and wisdom into the mix.

So without experience or money, Phil and I made the decision to take a leap of faith and start an international standard film festival in the small country town we'd recently moved to. This festival would be a cog in the wheel of our bigger vision to raise awareness about the power of life-enhancing films. All films at this festival had to add value to people – maybe laughter, maybe inspiration, maybe hope. We dreamed of a festival that would honour filmmakers rather than celebrities and would be a channel for distributing these special films around the world. We also wanted to support and train filmmakers in order to help them bring beautiful stories to the screen.

There wasn't anything saccharine about the content as you might expect with a 'positive film festival'. The sort of content we were looking for had to have something wonderful to say and to say it in fresh, creative ways.

We dreamed of a festival so amazing the world would flock to this event and that those attending would have an extraordinary experience. I remember one film distributor coming the first year and telling me, 'This is what church should be like'.

We trialled our first screening to a packed house in June 2005 and knew, that night, we were on the right track. We immediately made firm plans and set short and long term goals.

In October of that first year we formed a not-for-profit organisation and established a board. The first event ran 12 months later. Australia's favourite film critic, Margaret Pomeranz, said of the festival, 'This is magical. It's like there are no egos here. I've never experienced anything like it'.

And it *was* as though this festival was touched with magic. Michael Leunig designed our T-shirt and, even in the first year, filmmakers came from around the world. Famous artists donated work to our annual fund-raising art auction. More than 900 people entered our inaugural international photographic competition that we started to raise both money and the festival's profile. Our jury members were the cream of Australian cinema and our meals at the Awards Dinner were cooked by the best of chefs. All this was done on a shoestring through the generosity of many.

I felt as if I'd found what I was born to do. There was a huge sense of being exactly where I was meant to be. Who knew I could do this? Not me. I'd had no experience managing events. It was as though every skill I'd ever had suddenly came together and formed a big, beautiful bow. Do you ever have the feeling one day you'll arrive in your life? That one day everything will make sense? It all made sense. This was me. I'd arrived!

It's a great feeling when you find yourself, even if it's only temporarily.

My time was almost totally consumed with the festival which meant I effectively walked out of the business Phil and I had run together for more than 15 years. This left Phil carrying our family business alone and, while we'd decided together on this course of action, the impact of a doubled workload was huge for him. Additionally the financial impact of me leaving our business was significant. However, none of this stopped Phil backing our vision to the hilt. He volunteered his broad range of talents to help the festival and put in around 1,000 hours each year on the event.

Concurrent to our main event, we ran a family festival and also a schools' film festival. We housed all the attending filmmakers together and, by the third year, we ran 'Film Camp' before each festival where 'top-of-their-field' teachers taught the filmmakers.

One of the best things I created was the 'Screener Groups'. These started with about 20 people and grew each year until we had almost 100 regular 'screeners'. I had two objectives in mind when I started these weekly groups. Firstly, to involve the community, spread the word and grow a group of volunteers who were deeply knowledgeable about the films and the event. Secondly, I wanted to 'test run' every film before an audience. Each week, in various houses, submitted films would be screened and voted on.

'Screener Groups' met for six months of the year and became like family to each other. The first year I literally went down the street and invited random strangers to be part of this new thing. And strangers came!

We had groups who were so diverse they were hilarious. Among the group who met at our home there was a professor of maths, a young male tech genius, a pathologist, a French cheese-maker, an avocado farmer and a really sweet young couple who made porn for a living. They were all gorgeous people who didn't judge each other. It was the best of times. These wonderful 'screeners' became our friends, our devoted volunteers, our team who made the festival hum with love.

Every year the festival ran in the black, like clockwork and audience complaints were as rare as hens' teeth. In one year we achieved a staggering 193 newspaper and magazine articles, some international, and that's not counting all the TV and radio interviews. The director of one of the top film festivals in the world told me even he would struggle to have that sort of dream PR success. The fact that my sister, Ang, was one of Australia's best PR people and, for a time, donated her considerable skills, did have a lot to do with it.

Ang and I were the story-making duo no one could stop. We hit many of the goals Phil and I had set much earlier than anticipated:

It doesn't hurt that everyone who meets Ang adores her

To be featured on ABC's Australian Story within three years – it happened at our first event. The crew turned up and witnessed a miracle unfold.

National touring within three years – it happened the second year. We approached Hoyts Cinemas and toured a selection of the festival films around the country.

International recognition within five years – it happened sooner. In our third year, hugely popular Oscar nominated UK filmmaker Chris Jones named our festival as one of the best he'd ever attended. Filmmakers were talking and our reputation was growing rapidly.

WORLDS CRUMBLING

Just four years after I started work on the festival, our beautiful dream turned into a nightmare when my time as director came to an abrupt and unexpected end. To see this exceptional festival relinquished into other hands was heartbreaking. Relationships broke, horrible stuff happened and the domino effect eventually cost us our business. That domino effect continued and I won't bore you with details, suffice to say that I did little but cry and moan for a year. I'll tell you the story in the next chapter.

Two short years after we left the festival, when we had barely struggled to our feet again, some of our nearest and dearest closed the door on us. This is a situation I'm not at liberty to discuss. It was a journey into new territory where, by comparison, all previous pain was insignificant. For years it felt like my skin had been peeled away – the sort of pain there isn't really words for.

What was behind these two relationship breakdowns? I wanted to know and to find out if I could have done things better. Both these situations had me asking questions of myself and examining my behaviour. Neither of them made sense to me and I really couldn't work out what had gone wrong.

WHY, WHY, WHY?

I have a strong need to understand why. Why, why, why? I'm always asking why. This need has landed me in trouble in the past because, for some reason, most people, especially bosses and teachers, prefer you to just do as you're told.

I'm interested in gaining insight, in 'aha' moments. I'm interested in growth and I'm most interested in simple, practical ways to facilitate that growth.

This book is about me asking questions, finding answers and learning science and then mushing it into my life. Ideas and theories can be wonderful but sometimes they don't translate well to actual life. The things I share in this book are the things that worked for me.

When I discover some cool, amazing answer or some significant 'aha', my first response will usually be to tell someone about it. The urge to share what I learn is compelling.

And boy did I have a few 'aha' moments!

Along with 'Why?' I usually ask 'How?'. I have to understand how something works before I can get on board with it. Someone telling me to 'think positive' won't change my behaviour Someone explaining how postive thoughts change the way my brain processes information however, is an entirely different matter - that's life changing.

THE NEW FRONTIER

Gaining some understanding of how my brain works has been critical for me on so many levels. It has given me some freedom around a whole range of issues that were keeping me prisoner and this, in turn, released a good deal of the pain that had gathered through the ins and outs of my relationships. Just a simple shift in understanding can change so much.

What a feeling!

Our brains are ridiculously complex and studied by scientists from a range of disciplines. There isn't really one narrow field called *'Brain Science'* as I used to think. Research into which part of the brain does what is continually evolving and frequently the subject of debate and dispute. There are disagreements between fields of science and disagreements between scientists in the same field. And no wonder, some of these fields encompass many disciplines including some that are astounding, elaborate, and relatively new.

Take neuroscience for example. It began to come into its own only in the 1950s. Neuroscience is a broad field of biology that includes anatomy, biochemistry, molecular biology as well as the study of neurons. It also incorporates other fields such as psychology, mathematics, pharmacology, physics and engineering.

What I read in one book might well be quite different to what I read in another, and that's understandable because new frontiers are being explored. The brain is wild, weird and wonderful. No one person will ever be able to understand it.

This is the wild west and gold is only just starting to be found. I can't wait to hear what they'll discover next. So I keep asking why and how. And the wonderful world of brain science keeps delivering significant 'aha' moments. I'm hooked on brain science.

IT'S THAT SIMPLE

It's not only brain science that I find interesting, there's nothing I love more than a study about how people behave. I've always been a tad obsessed with finding out why people do things, how they live their lives and what makes them tick. I probably took my interest a little too far because more than once people have thought I was interrogating them and asked me if I was with the police!

Imagine my delight in finding a study that asked the question 'What makes for a good life?' It was right up my alley. Then imagine my extra delight when I found out this study had been going nearly 80 years! The icing on the cake was discovering there was a book about it by George E . Vaillant called *'Triumphs of Experience'*, and the book reads like a piece of poetry. I thought I was in heaven.

Then I actually *was* in heaven when I read that the main finding of this whole study, published and announced after 75 years, 268 men, thousands of tests, 20 million dollars and analysis of probably zillions of bits of data was:

'The good life is made with good relationships.'

The good life is made with good relationships. The good life is made with good relationships. The good life is made with good relationships. Did you read that? The good life is made with good relationships! I wanted to sing it.

It was that simple. It is that simple.

I love simple.

The study I'm referring to is Harvard's '*Grant Study*'. It's the longest longitudinal study of its kind in the world and is still running today. Harvard began recruiting men for the study in 1938 and during the next few years continued to recruit until they had 268 men. Less than 20 of the original cohort are alive at the time of writing this book. Most of the men remained with the study until their deaths. The attrition rate was very small because, according to *'Triumphs of Experience'* there were exceptional people staffing the study. John F. Kennedy was one of the original recruits and many famous and successful men also participated. This study delivers, and still delivers, many gems. I found *'Triumphs of Experience'* a riveting read.

Especially encouraging were the examples of men who started out narcissistic and thoughtless yet ended up men of honour and capable of great unselfishness.

The amount of data about physical and mental health gathered by the '*Grant Study*' is astonishing. The study is in-depth and involves both personal and written interviews, detailed health checks and later on, all kinds of new medical technologies were introduced. This study looks at triumphs and failures in both career and marriage and, at various times, focused on alcoholism and smoking.

In time the families of the men began to be included in the interviews and the research went on to include children and grandchildren of those men. Today more than 1,300 offspring of the original men are a formal part of the cohort. The study is, because of this aspect, unusually rounded and all the more fascinating.

HAPPIER AND HEALTHIER

One statement from the current study director, Robert Waldinger, backed up so much of what I'd been looking at:

> *'Good relationships keep us happier and healthier. Period.'*

The *'Grant Study'* findings indicate good relationships protect our brains from dementia and are better predictors of longevity at age 50 than cholesterol levels. It found that loneliness kills us and quality relationships are a key to longevity. Robert Waldinger was surprised by what the study uncovered:

'The surprising finding is our relationships, and how happy we are in our relationships, has a powerful influence on our health. Taking care of your body is important, but tending to your relationships is a form of self-care too. That, I think, is the revelation.'

The '*Grant Study*' isn't the only study showing the link between happiness and good relationships.

Professor Shawn Achor, formerly of Harvard, did his own studies:

> *'Turns out, there was one – and only one – characteristic that distinguished the happiest 10 percent from everybody else: the strength of their social relationships. My empirical study of well-being among 1,600 Harvard undergraduates found a similar result social support was a far greater predictor of happiness than any other factor, more than GPA, family income, SAT scores, age, gender, or race.'*

And, big relief, I don't have to be slim, beautiful or climb Mt Everest

The above quote is from Shawn's book '*The Happiness Advantage*', one you'll love if you're interested in being happier. All we have to do is learn how to have good relationships and it's instant admission to the good life. Of course the kind of good life I'm talking about has nothing to do with fame or a big bank account. We don't have to create great art, have a large house, own an expensive car, travel overseas, or get ahead. We're already ahead if we create great relationships. It doesn't matter if you didn't earn a degree, get into *Who's Who* or invent something fabulous. It doesn't even matter if you didn't marry, are childless, divorced or were adopted.

It also doesn't matter if, up to now, you haven't had great relationships because if this study shows one thing clearly, it's that it's never too late to start, never too late to learn.

MAKING THE GOOD LIFE

What I love is how I can take what I learn from all this science and make simple practical changes to enhance my life. The more relationship-wise I get, the more enjoyable my life is becoming.

These things have improved my life and my relationships, especially the one I have with myself. I now have more of the good life I was after.

My excitement about all I had learned eventually turned into popular and eye-opening workshops that I present all across the country in all sorts of places from schools and universities to small business, councils, government departments and also the largest of corporates. I adore doing workshops, events and speaking. However there are limits to my time; I can't do an endless number. I'm also frequently asked by workshop attendees how their son, father, boss, partner, friend or cousin might get hold of this material, and until now I've given them a very long list of books.

Now I'll be able to say 'Well funny you should ask, I happen to have a book about that'.

A book I wrote for everyone who struggles in any relationship. It's a book for everyone who wants to understand themselves, and others more, and get clear on what's happening when relationships aren't working well.

It's also a book for everyone who wants to make their good relationships even better because it's filled with deceptively simple tools that give you ways to bring more magic into ordinary days.

And now you, dear reader, have my book in your hands - I am so happy to be able to share with you these real-life stories along with all the simple practices I've learned.

I hope you find them as useful as I have.

PRACTICE

There'll be things to do

At the end of all chapters I'm going to suggest a 'practice'. Read the practice as it will have something important to contribute to the chapter. Your relationships will very likely improve if you take it one step further and actually practise the practice.

For this chapter the only practice I'm going to suggest is that you keep reading because there's some gold in this book. With 16 practices in total you'll have a few choices. Choose those that appeal and make sense to you.

I suggest you start with just one. You don't want to overwhelm yourself do you?

'And yet
it is the unknown
with all its
disappointments
and surprises
that is the most
enriching.'

ANNE MORROW LINDBERGH

THE GIFT FROM THE SEA

2

NOT MUCH OF A CATCH

My mother tells me I was almost born on The Sydney Harbour Bridge and 18 years later I was reborn, in a way, living right beside it. Reborn in the sense that I escaped the life I was in and entered a new world. I was living in a share house in Lavender Bay, Sydney. We'd sit on the deck and gaze at the bridge above us, a great pastime for anyone and a surreal one for those ingesting lots of drugs. And we were doing just that, taking dangerous amounts of dangerous drugs. I'd been doing it for years.

One night a friend arrived back from overseas with an expensive new sound system and a Joan Armatrading album. As he told me about his travels, and we listened to the sublime sounds of that album on a top level system, I realised I was missing out on life. I realised if I kept going with this narrow life of drugs and bridge-gazing I wouldn't live long and I'd never get to travel or experience the things my friend was talking about. Nor, almost more importantly at the time, would I ever get to own a sound system like that one.

A girl has to have her priorities straight!

A few days later the police knocked on the door asking for me. They'd found my bag that I'd managed to misplace on a rare trip outdoors. Rather than be overjoyed my bag was back, I was terrified. I knew what was in that bag. Fortunately for me those were the days before photo ID. I told the police that Toni was away for a few days and suggested they return when she was back. I packed my suitcase and fled.

Yes, I was quick on my feet that day

Was the police visit a nudge from the 'powers-that-be' or just a lucky coincidence? I have no idea. Either way, I left the drugs in Sydney and somehow landed a job wrangling unbroken horses on a farm outside Canberra. There was a farmhouse on the property shared by a group of young guys and a room in that house came with the job.

Drug-wise, the farm was relatively safe territory for me in that the guys in the house only smoked dope and drank quite a lot. Which meant I ended up, for a time, drinking quite a lot too. I hadn't really done much drinking up until then, drugs had been my thing.

One of the guys, Curly, apparently nicknamed because of his very long straight black hair, was heading into town one day and asked if I wanted to get out of the house. I didn't have a car, or even a driver's licence, so I grabbed the chance. Curly wanted to drop in and pick up some jewellery from his silversmith friend, a visit he promised would take just a few minutes. Those few minutes changed the course of my life.

A PASSING FANCY

I was nursing a post-party injury, so my ankle was bandaged. I limped across the lawn to where an older couple, the parents of the silversmith as it turned out, sat on their front verandah. The father stood up and called out a greeting to Curly then enquired of me, 'Oh my dear, what happened to you?'

'I got drunk and fell in a hole,' I replied.

This answer didn't endear me to them. It did, however, endear me to their son. Phil had been working under his VW station wagon and heard what I'd said. He was delighted that someone was so frank with his conservative parents and jumped up to see who it was. We took one look at each other and something happened. He saw a girl with an honest answer, courage and integrity. I saw a blond surfie with long hair, a hot guy, a conquest, a passing fancy. We were opposites attracting right in front of his parents who only saw in me a hippie, a druggie, and a danger to their son. They were not impressed.

For the next few months, we got together as frequently as his job allowed, often in the back of that VW and while it was fun and he was cute, I had no illusions that this was anything but a temporary fling.

One positive pregnancy test changed all that.

This was 1977, the tail-end of an era where teenagers were packed off to homes for unwed mothers. Being unmarried and pregnant was still frowned upon. Phil responded, as many good men did at the time, by proposing to me.

NOT MUCH OF A CATCH

As you'll have read in chapter one my response to his proposal wasn't what he expected. It was a ridiculous suggestion. Marriage hadn't even crossed my mind. I was 19 for goodness sake and marriage hadn't ever been high on my list of things to do. In fact it had never been on my list at all. I can't recall a single time I had dreamt of weddings, or babies or a settled life in the suburbs. I wanted to do exciting stuff and change the world. The thought of a traditional life working, working, working until retirement and being endlessly responsible was completely uninviting. I also had other baggage that may have influenced why marriage hadn't been on my radar. Apart from my dad and one male friend Mark, I hadn't really met men worthy of trust.

Mark is still my dear friend and is helping edit this book- hurrah.

Two violent rapes and a string of awful relationships had left me broken and suspicious. To me he was a sweet guy with a nice body. I simply hadn't thought further than that.

A couple of days after this insane proposal I was confiding in my girlfriend Donna. She was wise for her age, honest, frank and wonderful. I think I was hoping for comfort, backup, some sort of support.

What I got was the best advice I've ever had.

'That idiot asked me to marry him,' I scoffed. I expected her to laugh at the sheer lunacy of this idea. Maybe we'd have a bit of fun mocking him before we got down to the business of what on earth I was going to do next.

Instead Donna said, 'You're the idiot. He's wonderful. He would look after you every day of your life. You'll never get another offer like this one. Toni, you've got to face it, you're not much of a catch.'

I know! Not something you expect a friend to tell you.

On one level I was humiliated, shocked and angry at Donna for her bluntly delivered appraisal. Yet at the same time she opened my eyes to the truth. Phil was a catch and the smart thing to do would be to take him up on his offer.

It sounds crazy. It was irrational, yet somehow I knew she was right. He was the one. I still have no idea how I knew this, I just 'deep down' did.

So I accepted his proposal. His parents were horrified. They'd banned me from their home long before he proposed. I was just some 'bike' who was messing with their son.

I went on to have a good relationship with his lovely parents - eventually.

While my parents were supportive and caring, doing all they could to help, I do recall my mum saying, 'He's too good for you'. My mum insists she didn't make that comment.

Stay tuned, we'll be coming back to this mis-remembering later.

At the wedding, just six weeks later, people placed bets on how long our relationship would last. Some people refused to congratulate us.

There were two things they hadn't bet on. Well three really, though I can't tell you about the third for a while, so try to be satisfied with two. Firstly, we both had a lot of 'I told you so' coming our way if we messed up. Never underestimate the power of needing to prove people wrong.

Secondly, I'm the sort of person who puts my whole heart into anything I do and promises are very important to me. If I say 'yes' to you, then you're stuck with me. I will do absolutely anything I can to make it work and I want it to work well. I don't cut corners, I give it my best. I'll walk away only if I've tried everything. I've no idea where it comes from, it's just who I am. I think it's what Phil likes best about me, well that and my straightforward style.

So, despite what it looked like to outsiders, we weren't in this for the short term. The choice before us was: to live together miserably or find ways to make it work.

CONSULTING THE EXPERTS

During the next dozen years we were on a deliberate mission to find out how happy marriages happened. In a way the fact that I didn't love Phil turned out to be helpful because we weren't under any illusions this was going to work on its own. We, more than anyone, knew help was needed. We had broad social lives that put us in contact with a wide range of people. All the time we were on the alert for couples who were happy.

We were especially alert to older couples who were still dear friends with each other, who still held hands.

These were the experts and we'd 'consult' them by quizzing them about the details of their relationship. We'd ask for their secrets, for their wisdom and, most of all, for any practical advice. We read books, went to talks and did our best to incorporate what we were learning.

Donna had been absolutely right, Phil was a special man. A man unusually devoid of the fear that seems to plague us all – 'What will people think?' It simply never occurs to him. He doesn't care and this gives him rare bravery to do things that go against the grain, aren't stereotypical and might not fit with how people think someone should behave. Back then I didn't know many guys who'd have been willing to search out the secrets of good relationships, yet for Phil it was fascinating stuff. Even today he still loves talking about the complex world that is human relationships.

I'm happy to say that these days I know lots of guys who've worked out where the good life comes from and who are keen to explore what's been, historically, a more feminine realm.

NOW THE BAD NEWS STORY

Just after the March 2009 film festival ran, I was asked to prepare an operations manual so the festival could still run in the event something happened to me. This seemed like a brilliant idea and a woman was hired to interview me at length so that the many things only I knew about the festival would be accessible. Other key volunteers were also interviewed about their roles.

Almost immediately after the operations manual was finished I received an email that just about stopped my heart. It was a new plan of management for the festival that would have me reporting to multiple volunteer groups as well as the board. A plan that would make an already highly stressful and overwhelmingly huge job move into the realms of impossibility.

As soon as I read the email I knew my time was up. The urgency to create the operations manual, something the board had thrown around for years, suddenly took on a new light. This was confirmed when I talked to the Chairman of the Board. I asked her why she'd chosen to get rid of me and she answered, 'We have to protect the interests of our stakeholders'. I was stunned to find after founding the event and putting in 60-80 hour weeks for four years, on a mostly voluntary basis, I wasn't even considered a stakeholder. And, frustratingly, even after asking I was still none the wiser about the real reason for her actions. My cry to the board, since the first event ran, had been to move toward paid staff for the main day-to-day jobs. It was a much bigger job than two part-time people could manage.

From my point of view I felt, in order to have a consistent professional outcome and the growth Phil and I envisioned, we needed to have people with appropriate experience filling the key roles and have them working full-time.

Our volunteers were wonderful, hardworking and many had extraordinary talents yet there is only so much time you can demand of a volunteer. Working all week, week in and week out wasn't what most volunteers had the option to do.

In the months leading up to that email, I'd been working toward getting large sponsors for the festival. To do that we needed to convince those interested in sponsoring that we had sufficiently experienced people both in key roles at the festival and on the board. I'd had feedback from potential sponsors that there needed to be either event or film professionals in decision-making roles if we were to be taken seriously.

I had spoken of this to the board and I'd been sounding out interest from well-known professionals in the film industry to see if I could get two or three of them interested in being on the board. Incredibly, much loved Aussie film icons Noni Hazelhurst and Peter Thompson, were both open to getting involved. They'd already attended the festival as jury members and loved it.

However, when I saw that email I knew this new system was one I couldn't work with. It also told me the board wasn't going to pursue the course that would give us the opportunity to attract significant sponsorship. The sponsorship was essential for the festival to grow beyond a regional event and achieve the vision we'd founded it for. The proposed new system of management would be very unwieldy and I couldn't see how the festival could flourish under it.

The fact I felt pushed into a corner and resigned was no surprise to those board members behind the new plan. It seemed to me, from my conversation with the Chairman, and later other board members, they knew exactly what I'd do. I was terribly upset and felt betrayed because no one had discussed any of this with me personally.

Finding out one of the board members backing the new plan was someone I had trusted and confided in, someone I'd thought of as a friend, was a further blow that knocked the breath out of me.

I know not everyone on the board was behind the new management plan. The only board member who'd had international, or large project experience, was overseas for months while all this was going on. When he came back he resigned in outrage over how I'd been treated.

I offered to stay a month to help with hand over and tie up what remained to be done post the March event. One day I returned to the festival office to find a workman changing the locks on the office door and the Chairman of the Board with my laptop in her hand. As it was my own personal computer, that I had purchased with my own money, I was shocked to find her trying to take it.

In the first year after leaving the festival I was in a terrible mess. Initially I think I was in shock. We just hadn't seen this ending coming. It was a bombshell. Of course my sister Ang wrote the required media release saying I was leaving because of exhaustion and she wasn't lying. I was beyond tired after those four years. I knew my role directing the festival would now be an even bigger uphill battle and I simply didn't have the energy left to make that sort of climb, especially when some of the board seemed to be headed up a different hill altogether.

As we'd invented and designed this event, Phil and I owned all the Intellectual Property for the festival. We could easily have stomped our feet, acted vengefully and finished the festival completely or moved it to another location. However, this action wouldn't have been congruent with the spirit of the event. We handed over our IP to the remaining board on the proviso the festival continued to run. We sold our house, closed our business and left town. It was too painful to stay.

Hurt feelings and confusion aside, by far the biggest thing we both struggled with, was knowing that the vision we'd had for the festival would not now happen. The event would continue but the huge international potential would not be realised and we had failed to achieve the outcomes we'd envisaged. This vision was what had made the long hours, stress and financial sacrifice seem worthwhile and to see it come to an end was a severe blow. This was a loss that we mourned for years.

The board member I had thought was a friend said something to me on the day of our final board meeting. We were there to formally hand over our IP and we felt like we were handing over our baby. She said, 'Toni, we're doing this for you'. Her comment confirmed what I already knew from my conversation with the Chairman. This had been a planned ousting. I was already furious and this comment enraged me further because presenting that particular series of events as a 'favour' seemed outrageous.

I was to change my mind later, and I'll tell you more about that in another chapter.

The initial mix of anger, shock, hurt and shame dissipated into general misery that was punctuated occasionally by nasty, vengeful thoughts. I'd imagine certain board members falling under a bus or off a cliff or some other such tragedy. After a year I thought the only lesson I could take away from our time there was not to trust again. Ever!

It turns out that 'Do not trust' was not the main lesson. It wasn't the lesson at all.

THE GIFT OF QUESTIONS

It's totally nauseating when someone has something awful happen to them and then afterward they bounce up out of the ashes and say, 'Oh it was such a gift... blah, blah'.

They tell you all about how their tragedy was the making of them, that they learned something incredible and how, in the long run, it was the best thing that could have happened to them. I know, intensely irritating! However, while I hate to disappoint you, you'd better prepare to be somewhat nauseated because I'm about to tell you that now, years later, I can see what happened was a gift and I did learn incredible things.

I had so many questions about what had happened. I was unsure if my behaviour or personality had been the issue. I wondered why our version of events didn't match the version of events being circulated by some. I wanted to know why I'd behaved as I had and why some of the others involved had behaved the way they had. I was desperate to understand and I discussed these questions endlessly with Phil and our close friends.

ANOTHER CATASTROPHE

As I mentioned in chapter one, two years after the festival catastrophe, some close relationships broke down unexpectedly. It seemed everything we did to try and repair the connections only made things worse. We had to accept the loss of what we'd once had. After this happened I was back asking the same sort of questions as I had after the festival. Except now the answers were much more important.

These two 'catastrophes' ended up being of great service to me because they forced me to ask the big questions. These questions made me confront things, grow, take responsibility and more closely examine who I was and my role in the outcome of these relationship breakdowns. I've had to learn more about why people do what they do and why I do what I do.

A hide and seek game for you.

I've found answers to some of my questions and they're threaded through this book. Before we get to any answers though, I've posed some questions for you to ponder in the next chapter called, not surprisingly, The Questions.

PRACTICE

The Bad Equals Good List

Make a list of all the tough stuff that's happened in your life and then see how many of these things ended up being, in some way, wonderful. Then you can also make others nauseated. Won't that be fun?

'There are four
questions of value in life,
Don Octavio.
What is sacred?
Of what is the spirit made?
What is worth living for and
what is worth dying for?
The answer to each is the same.
Only love.'

LORD BYRON

3

THE QUESTIONS

You might be wondering why finding answers matters so much to me. Why don't I just move on, chalk it up to experience and forget it. I can't. I don't know why I'm a 'why' person, I just am.

I'm convinced that who you are in the world matters; how you do life matters; and most of all, how you do relationships matters.

Things had gone wrong. I wanted to make sure I wasn't making the same mistakes again and I was convinced that finding answers to some of the questions coming up would help me navigate, and keep, the relationships I had. I wanted to know why we blame, why apologies are hard to come by, why stories change and how memory works.

I wondered why we're reluctant to take responsibility for the things we do and why we may not even notice what we've done to someone else. I was curious as to why people don't want to talk about emotionally difficult stuff, aren't honest with each other and go behind each other's backs. I wanted to know why we see things so differently, tell different stories about the same events and justify our own behaviour. I needed to understand how seemingly good people can also be cruel when it suits them. I was interested in why, since we all mess up, we're so defensive and want to cover things up when we've made mistakes. I also wanted to know why I do what I do and say what I say. And I've always wanted to understand why I can react in ways that are over the top if things get emotional. There was also another hope that maybe, if I understood myself and others better, I could lay to rest some of the things that hadn't gone well in previous relationships.

I was right to think that understanding some of these things might help me. It's made a big difference to my ability to get on top of my emotions, resolve past issues, let go of crap and a host of other things including a big improvement in how I feel about myself, all of which have a profound impact on how I do relationships.

And what's not to love about that?

I'll be posing versions of these questions in this chapter and I've set them in true situations. The answers to the questions will be found in subsequent chapters of this book.

TWO FRIENDS

My friend Merridy is a bit of a music nut, which is one of the reasons I love her. We share some similar loves. Merridy has worked, among other incredible jobs, as a music programmer for radio stations. She's played professionally in bands and been involved in a number of ways in the music scene. Music is her thing, just as it was her father's thing. Her treasured possession is her vinyl collection and her most treasured of that collection are the records she inherited from her father.

Some years ago Tania, a close friend of Merridy's, was celebrating a very special anniversary. Tania was a former ballroom dancer and as a surprise, she was whisking her husband off to a hideaway where some of their oldest friends from their dancing past had agreed to meet for a weekend away together. Tania asked Merridy if she could, please pretty please, borrow a selection of her vinyl records for the weekend. Tania was especially keen to have the older ones from her dad's collection, such as Nat King

Cole. While Merridy wasn't keen to have her records out on loan, or even out of her house, she reluctantly agreed. When her friend arrived to pick them up Merridy reminded her, 'These were my dad's, please be careful with them'.

Listen to your gut Merridy, this isn't going to end well!

You can guess what happened. When Tania returned the albums some weeks later she said they'd had a lot of fun on their weekend, thanked Merridy, and left. On further examination, Merridy found some of the records had deep scratches, two of the covers were stained and one was ripped. When Merridy called her friend and outlined the state of the albums Tania said, 'I'm sorry, it was a big weekend. Look I'll get you an iTunes voucher – that should cover it'.

Of course Merridy was heartbroken and dismayed. She couldn't understand how Tania could be so heartless. Tania didn't acknowledge that Merridy had lost something precious through her actions or seem to care that Merridy was upset. In fact Tania demeaned the value of what Merridy had lost by her insulting offer of an iTunes voucher.

Merridy was angry with Tania. She felt as though her friend had been careless not only with her records but also with the friendship. Later Merridy called Tania and explained how she felt only to be told, 'I don't know why you let this sort of stuff bother you so much Merridy. You get uptight easily don't you?'

So my first question is:

> *'Why didn't Tania understand that her behaviour towards Merridy was thoughtless and unkind?'*

A HAPPY FAMILY

Phil and I know a family who seemed to be the happiest of all the families we knew. Devoted parents with gorgeous kids, some of whom were already responsible teenagers when a devastating event happened. The dad, Paul, who we know well, is a pillar of the community, very involved in his church, hard-working, funny, and unusually generous. He'd been incredibly supportive to us through a few tough times. We have great respect for this man and he obviously adored his wife.

We also knew many of Paul's friends all of whom held him in the same high esteem we did. These friends were all as shocked as we were when one day, with no warning, Sarah walked out on Paul and her children and went off to live with a younger man.

I actually find it difficult to convey just how gobsmacked we all were when Sarah left. This was a very spiritual couple with a strict moral code. They were very family-focused, had a thriving business, they solved conflicts well, there wasn't any obvious marital tension, and nothing that looked even close to an ongoing issue. There was no violence or abuse, and they'd never needed to seek counselling about their relationship. Paul believed they were *very* happily married.

No one could believe it, and no one, including Paul, saw any indication that this would happen. I've known plenty of husbands who hadn't seen it coming when a wife leaves. In each case everyone around them could see the issues even when those husbands didn't. This situation was very different.

We all found it so difficult to process, that we tried to find a reason to explain Sarah's baffling behaviour. In every way this was totally unlike her. We decided it had to be a brain tumour. Her reasoning had to be impaired. Or maybe it was a momentary chemical attraction that had swept her away and she'd soon come to her senses and return home. It was neither of these two reasons. Sarah didn't come home and she wasn't ill.

Sarah had just decided to chuck her family, her religion and her previous moral standards and start a new life.

In fact, instead of coming home to her children and heartsick husband, she began a series of vicious lawsuits against him. Fourteen lawsuits in just eight years. Each of these lawsuits attacked Paul's character. She went through the whole gamut of possible crimes including accusing him of lying, hiding money and being threatening to her. She even threw a Domestic Violence Order at him, something I think nearly broke him. As soon as one lawsuit was settled in his favour (always), she'd launch into another. Her trouble was that she couldn't come up with evidence for any of her accusations. Despite this, it was clear Sarah was blaming Paul for her actions in a very big way.

My question is:

> *'Why is Sarah attacking Paul for what was her decision?'*

AN AMERICAN PRESIDENT

George Bush ended his career with a very low popularity rating and even his brother wanted to distance himself from him. The main reason being the Iraq War debacle. George Bush led America to war, spent loads of money and caused the deaths of many, based on a series of lies about Weapons of Mass Destruction.

One Keeps hoping leaders won't lie.

To quote Paul Waldman of *'The Week'*: 'In 2008, the Center for Public Integrity completed a project in which they went over the public statements by eight top Bush administration officials on the topic of Iraq, and found that no fewer than 935 were false, including 260 statements by President Bush himself.'

When no evidence of these weapons was found, despite a jolly good look, Mr Bush didn't hang his head in shame. Instead he crowed from the rooftops about his achievement. He even put up a banner – *Mission Accomplished!* His story isn't unusual. I could easily have selected any number of people in public life from all political persuasions. This isn't only a Republican thing. Bush's story is just a very extreme example. We see these situations not only in politics, it happens everywhere. Despite evidence to the contrary, people regularly refuse to admit they're wrong, so my next question is:

'Why didn't George Bush admit he was wrong?'

TEENAGERS AND PARENTS

In a study done by psychology professors Brooke Feeney and Jude Cassidy, teenagers and parents met in a lab where they were asked to answer a series of questions. The questionnaire covered the sort of things that can cause conflict in families, such as personal appearance, curfew, behaviour and boundaries. The questions also asked about the nature of the relationship the teens had with their parents. After the initial round of questions the teenagers then spent time alone with their parents to try to resolve their greatest area of disagreement.

Directly afterwards the teenagers were taken aside and asked to write down their answers to a series of questions about the attempted resolution they'd just had with their parents. They had to rate the conflict, as well as answer questions about their emotional response during the session with their parents. Six weeks later the teenagers came back and answered the exact same set of questions regarding the time spent trying to resolve the conflict with their parents.

Researchers noted that in the follow up questionnaire, the answers were often quite different to the ones they'd given originally. The study revealed the kids who were quite close to their parents, and got on well with them, remembered the interaction as being considerably less intense and conflicted than they had rated it six weeks before. Those kids who already had distant, difficult or ambivalent relationships with their parents tended to recall the conflict in a more negative way. On the second survey, six weeks after the event, these teenagers reported that the conflict was more angry and bitter than they'd related on the earlier questionnaire.

For this scenario my question is:

> *'Why are the teenagers remembering the same conflict so differently?'*

TWO COLLEAGUES

This is a story of two women, one of them is a good friend of mine. The other was once a colleague of hers.

My friend is funny and clever. She's into self-development; she meditates and we can talk for hours about a wide range of interesting topics. We can get deep, deep, deep. I love hanging out with her. In terms of qualities, she has many of the best. She's wise, generous, and kind. However, I can't reveal her true identity, so I'm going to call her Very Nice, Wise Caring Woman or Very Nice for short. The other woman in this story we'll call Arrogant, Control Freak Woman or Cruella for short. The less said about her the better. You can already tell what she's like.

Very Nice and I often meet for coffee. We laugh, catch up and solve the problems of the world. One day I was waiting in a coffee shop for Very Nice to meet me. She was running a tad late and when she finally arrived she wasn't her usual sunny self.

Very Nice was fuming. She was mad. She was very, very angry. I'd never seen her so upset and it didn't take long for her to tell me why. She'd come straight to our rendezvous from her workplace where something awful had just happened. Very Nice had been publicly humiliated in front of the whole office by, you guessed it, the evil Cruella. Cruella had yelled at Very Nice in earshot of all the other staff, had called Very Nice mean, controlling and aggressive. Very Nice was appalled, embarrassed and humiliated. She felt publicly shamed. By the time she got to me, just an hour later, her shame had turned to anger.

Boo, Cruella, boo to you!

I sat and listened while she told me all the details, and then told me again. That's what friends do, stay quiet and let each other unload until it's all out on the table. Once she was finished I asked her a question:

> *'Very Nice, can you tell me what you were doing or what was happening just before Cruella exploded?'*

Very Nice stopped talking and thought carefully. An expression of surprise crossed her face, then she looked aghast. 'Oh no!' she said.

Very Nice told me what had happened. It turned out that she had been, for some time prior to Cruella's outburst, deliberately and publicly pushing Cruella's buttons. Yes, my own Very Nice had started the ruckus.

Very Nice had the grace to look ashamed and told me she knew she needed to apologise to Cruella for her actions. The next time I saw Very Nice I asked her if she'd said sorry and was interested to hear that Very Nice had indeed apologised to Cruella. I then asked if Cruella had apologised to her. 'No, she didn't. She just seemed surprised it had taken me so long to realise the error of my ways,' said Very Nice.

So my last question is this one:

> *'Why didn't Cruella apologise to Very Nice?'*

Some of the answers will become apparent in the next chapter.

PRACTICE

The Explosion Exam

Has anyone ever just exploded at you? Yelled, screamed and said hurtful things to you? Think about those times. Ask yourself the question. I asked Very Nice, 'Can you tell me what you were doing or what was happening just before (*insert name*) exploded?'

This could be interesting.

‘We do not see things as they are. We see things as we are.’

THE TALMUD

4

BLIND SPOTS

I read a lot of books, though my unreliable memory ensures not many of them stay with me unless I take notes. John Medina's book, *'Brain Rules'* is one of the exceptional ones. In this book I learned many amazing things. However what I learned about vision and how we see was truly fascinating and eye-opening.

I hadn't realised that vision was, by far, our most dominant sense and that it trumps all others in terms of which of your senses your brain will pay attention to. Vision uses up half of your brain's total resources and the process of 'seeing' isn't as cut and dried as you may have thought.

I don't know about you but I've always thought my eyes were like cameras, taking 'fileable' little pics of exactly what was out there. I imagined tiny polaroids stacked up in my head, a safe record of all the real things I'd seen in my life. I'd say something was true, real and reliable because I had seen it. I'd seen it with my own eyes, therefore it must be true.

One of the many, many fascinating things Medina writes about is how you see. Medina says the information our eyes are receiving is *'incomplete and quite untrustworthy'*, which was somewhat of a shock to me at the time. I hadn't ever considered my sight to be untrustworthy before.

THE MINI MOVIES

Here's my basic version of Medina's explanation regarding how eyes work. To start the process your retina takes in the information from the outside world. That information becomes a collection of tracks that are essentially mini-movies and there can be up to 12 of those. The good old optic nerve whizzes this information through to the thalamus (your brain's distribution centre) and as it leaves the thalamus, it travels along hundreds of neural streams that become increasingly divided. Eventually there are thousands of streams taking the information about what you just 'saw' off to the visual cortex.

The way Medina describes the visual cortex as '*a large area of visual acreage with thousands of lots and each lot is ridiculously specific*'. He talks about how each lot responds to only particular things. One lot may only respond to a certain angle, or a certain colour, or even just a certain shade of orange. One might be responding to motion, another to checked patterns and another only to paisley designs.

Your brain then retrieves all these little bits of information and puts them in some sort of order. The visual cortex then sends that more refined information to the association area of your brain. Once the association area looks at everything, and further assembles the information, it makes a decision about what has been seen and, post decision, you 'see'.

How wild is this? It's amazing.

AN OPINION OF WHAT IS THERE

To complicate this even further, your retinas have blind spots. Actual places where no information gets in so your brain just makes an educated guess and fills in bits of the picture for you. A bit like some of the drawing programs you can get these days where the computer just fills it all in.

John Medina says:

> *'We actually experience our visual environment as a fully analysed opinion of what the brain thinks is out there.'*

This means everything you see is filtered through everything you already know before it even gets 'decided' on. Everything you've ever seen is influencing what you see today.

Yes, this was one of the 'aha's

The implication of this for relationships is huge. No matter how hard you try, you can never, ever see the same world that another person sees.

It isn't your eyes that 'see', it's your brain. Shawn Achor agrees:

> *'The reason some people see the world so differently from others is that the human brain doesn't just take a picture of the external world like a camera; it is constantly interpreting and processing the information it receives.'*

HALLUCINATING REALITY

I was listening to a fabulous TED talk recently by Anil Seth, a cognitive neuroscientist from Suffolk University, called '*Your Brain Hallucinates Your Concious Reality*'. It's a must see if this topic is interesting to you.

He calls the brain a 'prediction engine' and says that *'Perception has to be a process of informed guesswork in which the brain combines sensory signals with its prior expectation or belief about how the world is to form its best guess of what is out there in the world'*.

Seth maintains that we depend as much on the perceptual predictions that our brains make as on information coming into our brains:

'We don't just passively perceive the world, we actively generate it.'

Seth says our perception of what is out there in the world is controlled hallucination and when we agree about our hallucinations we call it reality.

He also points out the driving factor behind our sense of self is our brain making sure we stay alive.

Defensiveness is an integral part of staying alive and drives a good deal of our perception and interpretation of the world as well as explaining a lot of our behaviour.

DIFFERENT WORLDS

Is it any wonder that you don't see eye-to-eye with your parents? Is it any wonder you and your partner cannot seem to agree on how it really is? Is it any wonder your boss sees a six when you see a nine?

How can I go on demanding that you see it, do it, play it, behave it 'my' way, when you don't even see the same world I do? I can't because that would be unreasonable.

No matter how long I spend living with Phil, I'll never be able to see or experience the world as he does. His values, perceptions and a whole host of things remain completely unchanged despite all my attempts to convince him that my values are the 'right' ones. We were at a seminar recently and were asked to answer the question:

'If you had all the money in the world, all the time and all the help you needed with no restrictions what would you do with your life?' I didn't miss a heartbeat, I knew.

'I'd change the way people experience ageing,' I answered.

'I'd have chickens,' said Phil.

Proof that 40 years down the track no amount of me sharing my vision, taking action and being on various missions to 'change the world' has in any major way altered what is important to him. Also proof that 40 years down the track I still have no idea what he's going to say next.

It's a miracle anyone gets on at all let alone stays with one person for a lifetime. You may well find me saying that more than once in this book because, by the time I've finished it will seem even more of a miracle.

THE BUCKET

Even this morning we were both hysterical with laughter about how differently we see things and how little idea we really have of what the other might truly be thinking.

In the night I'd found a large bucket placed neatly next to our kitchen bin.

We live in an apartment and don't have a garden or a compost bin. However, a very good friend, Mary-Lou, had recently asked if we'd collect vegetable scraps for her compost. Of course we agreed and found a little container and hid it discreetly under the sink. We also had a larger one out in the carport. Perfect. Until last night.

I was pretty sure I knew what was going on. I suspected Phil wanted a larger receptacle in the kitchen so we didn't have to empty the little container all the time. 'Sensible' he'd have thought. 'Convenient' he'd have thought. 'Clever' he'd have thought.

If he was imagining I wouldn't notice a 20 litre bucket, then 'clever' didn't come into it.

So we had a little discussion about the bucket. I was trying to establish if my assumptions had been correct. Was he actually wanting a giant bucket to live in the kitchen? Having seen my reaction to the bucket he wasn't being all that forthright and was playing dodgem cars. 'Well, I just put it there for a minute, I was going to move it,' and other such tosh.

I should point out that after this length of time together we both know each other's games very well and they are a source of endless amusement.

I kept trying to pull him back to the real issue at hand. What I wanted to know was if he actually imagined our lives with a bucket in the kitchen? A bucket with big yellow words on it. A plasterer's bucket.

The 'WTF? there's a BUCKET in the Kitchen!' bucket.

Before I banished it to the carport I had to know if it was important to him to have it in the kitchen. Though how I'd handle living with the bucket if it was important to him I hadn't decided. So I tried a different tack. 'Okay Phil, stop laughing and tell me seriously, when Mary-Lou asked us to collect compost for her, what do you think was my first thought?'

'How wonderful it would be to help the environment?' he said.

I started howling with laughter. 'Oh my God, you've known me how long and you think that is my first thought? Really?' I care about the environment. I do. However, it wasn't my first, or even second thought. 'My first thought was how great it would be to have one little thing we could do for Mary-Lou when she spends most of her time kindly editing my book and I don't do anything for her. Do you want to know my second thought?'

If you can laugh and look worried at the same time that's how he looked after my question. 'Ummm…' He clearly had no idea so he hedged for a while then tried 'I don't know. Ah, um, do I?' he said.

'Yes you do. My second thought was "Oh no, I bet he'll get a giant bucket and put it in the kitchen" and you did!'

After we stopped laughing I tried again to get to the bottom of his desires about the bucket. He's so easy-going it's not hard to walk all over him and I was trying to figure it out, so I said, 'Okay, let's just imagine we're not married. I'm not here. If I'm completely out of the picture where do you want the bucket to live?'

'On a farm,' he said.

Despite the chicken comment a few weeks ago I was surprised again. We cried with laughter for ages.

YOUR VERY OWN ILLUSIONIST

As if retinal blind spots, hallucinations and filtering information through all our prior experiences wasn't bad enough we also have other more blinding blind spots. Psychological blind spots!

Your brain is quite the illusionist and one of its cleverest tricks is to utterly and absolutely convince you that you don't have any blind spots. None, nada, zilch.

Others however, well you can see their blind spots easily, their hypocrisy sticks out a mile. They have wrong-thinking. It's obvious. But you? No way. We really are quite blind to our blind spots and blind spots can and do have a huge effect on all sorts of areas of our lives including, obviously, our relationships.

MY PERSONALITY PROBLEM

I have a rather shocking personality problem. My problem is that I actually, truly, deeply, believe that I see things as they really are. And I believe my beliefs and actions are acceptable, reasonable and require little explanation as they are entirely normal. I haven't admitted this publicly before but part of this problem, that I've only recently realised I had, is I know, without doubt, my political beliefs are the ones people would hold if they only understood things as well as I do. I also know if only those involved with such things as climate change, war and other social issues would listen to me, I could give them the balanced view they are lacking and all of this could be worked out.

I also assume other people see things similarly to how I do, (the right way) and I think this right up until to the point when they disagree with me. That's when I know they aren't seeing things properly because if they were seeing things properly they'd agree with me.

What I think they need are more facts to enlighten them and then, I think, they'll agree with me. Sadly this affliction, this personality disorder, causes some awful traits in me. I can be so sure of my rightness I can be arrogant and so sure of your wrongness I become judgmental. I compare everyone to me and those who don't measure up are assessed accordingly.

Psychologists have a name for my terrible affliction. It's called naive realism. The prognosis is quite bad and it appears that being cured of it is unlikely.

However, before you rush to judge me, read on…I was listening to a brilliant podcast called *You Are Not So Smart* (episode 101) on this very disorder recently and they played a little piece of a comedy sketch by George Carlin that went like this:

> *'First a philosophical question: Have you ever noticed when you're driving that anyone driving slower than you is an idiot? And anyone driving faster than you is a maniac? Say, look at this idiot here, will you just look at this idiot? Look at that idiot just creeping along. Ooh, just look at that maniac go! I mean it's a wonder we ever get anywhere at all with all the idiots and maniacs there are because there is certainly no one driving at my speed.'*

Does this sound familiar? Carlin has made an astute observation. He's observed naive realism at work.

YOUR PERSONALITY PROBLEM

I'm thrilled I'm not alone in this.

Carlin's observations should sound familiar because everyone suffers the same delusions, the same shocking personality problem as I do. Naive realism with an overlay of blind spots.

Yes, I mean you too. Everyone is the same.

Lee Ross, Professor of Psychology at Stanford (since 1969) and leading-light on naive realism, tells how he's always loved freaking out his incoming students with his ability to accurately pinpoint their political views. He does this very scientifically by asking them to write down some crucial information: their star sign, their favourite colour and what animal they most like.

So, let's say his student, we'll call her Annie, tells him she loves red, is an Aries and has a pet cat. He would be able to tell her, with great assurance, that this was her political stance: 'You are as liberal as is reasonable, and people to the left of you politically are just a little too idealistic and those to your right are too callous and too selfish. You're in the sweet spot, you're as rational and reasonable as can be'. Annie would be amazed. He has nailed her in one. Though she's wondering how the cat came into it.

In truth the cat didn't come into it, nor did the star sign nor the colour. No matter which student Lee plays this game with, they are all amazed his assessment, the same one I just shared, is their own political stance.

We all think we are rational, reasonable and normal and anyone choosing differently to us is somehow lacking, probably wrong and, at very least, is too 'something'.

TOO SOMETHING

> *'She should put more clothes on. She's too skimpily dressed!'*
>
> *'That Green Party, they're too left-wing.'*
>
> *'They're too lenient. Their children are so badly behaved.'*
>
> *'Did you see what he had on? He's too old-fashioned. He needs to update his look.'*
>
> *'I'm worried about Fred. He's too rash with his money. I'd never buy a boat.'*
>
> *'That church? They're too liberal. I stopped going there.'*
>
> *'I think she's too greedy. Eight or 10 pairs of shoes I can understand, but 45?'*
>
> *'The climate-change people are too fearful, they're imagining things.'*
>
> *'Their diet is worrying, vegetarian would be ok, but vegan is taking it too far.'*

I can't tell you how many times I've tried to explain my reasons, my carefully thought out and convincing reasons, for something I believe or do, only to have them rejected by the person I'm explaining them to. Apparently this is a well-known part of the whole naive realism thing. We think if we explain the 'facts', then the other person has to come to our way of thinking, because obviously, this is the right way of thinking and they were just missing some facts. In reality those people to whom I subjected my 'right facts' have their own set of 'right facts' they'd like me to understand.

How many times have you done the same? This naive realism with a sprinkling of blind spots is, frustratingly, everywhere.

A STANFORD SANDWICH BOARD

Most of us think it's pretty easy to work out what other people are going to do or say. After all, we've been surrounded by other people all our lives and we know the way they work. Nope.

The truth is we all think other people think the same way we do. Guess what? They often don't. In fact our own biases can blind us to the way other people are going to think or act.

Professor Ross coined a phrase for one of these biases. He called it the False Consensus Effect and conducted a couple of studies in the late 1970s to explore it more fully. One of these studies, involving students being asked to wear a sandwich board advertising a coffee shop for a few hours, has become rather famous. About 50% of the students asked said yes to wearing the sandwich board, the rest said no, they didn't want to wear it. In the end no one actually wore a sandwich board because the point of the study was to hear what participants would say about the choices of other participants.

The study showed that most people assume others, given the same circumstances, would choose to do as they have done. The reason they assume this is because they rate their own choice as normal.

'Of course they'd wear the sandwich board, who wouldn't?'

Students were surprised to find others in the study had chosen differently to them. They invented reasons that explained, to themselves, why these students hadn't made the same choice as they did. On hearing students had refused to wear the sandwich board the ones that had agreed to wear it said things like, 'They must be afraid of looking like a fool.' or 'They can't have much of a sense of humour.'

When asked what reason they'd give to explain their own choice the students tended to say things along the lines of, 'Me? No reason, why would I need a reason? It's normal'. They were baffled their own decision could possibly need explanation.

If you start looking, asking questions and noticing, you'll find the same sort of comments everywhere.

Deep down, if people don't agree with you it will be likely you'll ascribe some sort of fault or shortcoming to their 'not-normal' decision.

Of course your own decision won't need explanation though. You are totally normal and everyone would understand your choice.

A RECIPE FOR DISASTER

And this brings me to the answer for the first question about the friends and the damaged vinyl records.

> Q: 'Why didn't Tania understand her behaviour towards Merridy was thoughtless and unkind?'
>
> A: Because Tania considered her behaviour normal and if Merridy had difficulty with her behaviour it was because Merridy was somewhat deficient or wrong.

Merridy is clearly too fussy, too anal, too attached to material things, too sentimental or any of a million little arrows Tania could sling. Tania doesn't have much attachment to things that belonged to her own parents and so her behaviour was in keeping with her values and seemed normal and right to her.

Naive realism is what's driving your opinions of those who disagree with you, and for the most part, you're entirely unaware of it.

Think about the implications for every single one of your relationships. In any conflict, if both parties are entirely convinced of their rightness, only one side will be happy with the outcome. Sure sometimes, for the sake of peace, you give in to their wrongness. However you still know you're right, and it smarts to have to give in to what you know is the wrong way.

HEAVEN'S GATE

All of these blind spots, biases and 'personality disorders' can get even sane, normal and rational people into huge difficulty. Once we're convinced of something we become unwilling to let it go even when there is evidence to the contrary. What happened in the *Heaven's Gate* community is a perfect, though tragic, example.

In 1997 members of the religious group, *Heaven's Gate*, committed suicide in order to rid themselves of their bodies. 39 people died, people who thought they wouldn't need their bodies because they believed a spaceship, that was following the soon-to-arrive *Hale-Bopp Comet*, was coming to take them to a new paradise. This group of people all willingly killed themselves, despite the fact that a few weeks prior to the anticipated pick-up time, the group purchased a high powered telescope in order to get a view of their coming chariot – the spaceship. They could see the Hale-Bopp Comet yet couldn't find the spaceship, so they returned the telescope to the shop they'd purchased it from. Their reason for the return? The telescope was faulty! Even evidence didn't deter them from their plans. Afterward friends and family were interviewed and, by all accounts, those that died were sane, smart and reasonable people. They were just terribly blind to anything that didn't fit with what they knew they definitely knew. Exactly the same as all of us.

THE LIGHT

So, to take stock, you have a brain that sees the world in an entirely unique way and the desire to keep you safe, alive and well is a big driver. You have a naturally defensive brain. Additionally your brain will hang on tightly to beliefs and has a huge need to be right. This same brain is convinced that you do, actually, truly, see things how they ***really*** are.

Right now your brain is probably going 'Well, duh! Yes, of course I do!'

I don't know about you but that seems to be a recipe for disaster and I don't want more disaster, I've created enough of that.

If I shine a bit of light on my blind spots I can see that I'm often wrong, can be cruel, am frequently selfish, don't know everything, can be lazy, distracted, and thoughtless. I do stupid things, make mistakes and can be unkind.

And if I'm really going to step into the light then I also have to own that sometimes the situations I would love to blame on someone else can be the direct result of my own behaviour.

It's very tempting to say things like: 'It's them. It's their stuff. It's not me. It's their problem. They're just projecting their pain on to me'

However I'm not going to learn anything or see things change simply pointing the finger.

Sometimes, like Very Nice, I've pushed the buttons that cause the blow up.

Yet I prefer not to step into the light. I prefer not to self-reflect because when I do I start feeling very uncomfortable. And it's this feeling I'll be examining in the next chapter.

PRACTICE

Get a Blind Spot Buddy

If you truly want to improve your relationships then get a blind spot buddy or two. A blind spot buddy is there to give you honest feedback and help you be aware of what it is you prefer not to see. Ask them to be brutal with you.

Ok, I know this isn't the easiest practice, and you don't want to destroy your relationship with your blind spot buddy so you'll need to be very brave and fight your desire to justify and explain to your buddy why you do see things the right way.

Have fun with that.

'Could
a greater miracle
take place than for us to
look through
each other's eyes
for an
instant?'

HENRY DAVID THOREAU

5

THE ASSASSIN OF LOVE

When I think about happiness, peace, satisfaction, enjoyment and then look at what interrupts those sort of good things, I usually find one main culprit.

Them.

They're the problem. Other people.They're the source of most of my pain.

THE PROBLEM OF THEM

When I'm feeling emotional pain my tendency is to look to others and feel they're the cause of my pain and therefore the problem. As this chapter explains, it's a very common tendency so it's likely to be exactly what you do too.

I blame them, point the finger at them and then run a whole lot of judgements and ascribe motives to their actions that have caused me pain. I'm sure I know what's behind what they said or did to me. I know what's driving them.

> *'Oh, she's just jealous. She's always like that, she's very insecure.'*
>
> *'They're very fussy you know. I bet they won't loan it to us because they're afraid we won't look after it.'*

> *'I'm sure he hates me, he's always rude to me whenever I go over. I think he doesn't really like women with opinions.'*
>
> *'She always goes on the attack. I think she has mother issues and I must remind her of her mother.'*

This is exactly what I did with the people on the board at the festival. I blamed them and then came up with all sorts of deep, dark motives that explained to me why they'd done what they'd done. And as what they'd done wasn't in keeping with what I'd do, or more accurately, what I thought I'd likely do in the same situation, then, they had to be wrong.

MISTAKES WERE MADE (but not by me)

However, I don't really know what is driving them. I'm blind, living in a different world from the board members, and every other friend or 'enemy' in my life. To top it off, as we already know, I have a blazing personality disorder.

Not only don't I know their motives, I don't even know my own.

My favourite ever non-fiction book is called '*Mistakes Were Made (but not by me)*' by renowned social psychologists Carol Tavris and Elliot Aronson. This is a book about how cognitive dissonance comes into play when we do silly, mean or dishonest things, how it blinds us and can affect our relationships as we try to shift blame. It's full of eye-openers like this one:

> *'In a sense dissonance theory is a theory of blind spots – of how and why people unintentionally blind themselves so that they fail to notice vital events and information that might make them question their behaviour or their convictions.'*

'Mistakes Were Made' is the book where I first learned about blind spots and heard about Lee Ross's work and much, much more. This book provided many of the answers I was looking for. Though not really a self-help book it allowed me entry into the world of understanding myself and others in a new and very helpful way. It's intriguing, well written and entertaining as well.

So what is this dissonance thing? It's when there is disharmony in your mind because you're holding opposing ideas or beliefs or actions.

Cognitive dissonance is the uncomfortable feeling you get when what you do or say doesn't quite match up to who you think you are or align with your beliefs.

Your brain doesn't like you to be on two ends of the see-saw at once so it produces discomfort to let you know there is something wrong. The discomfort is called cognitive dissonance.

I feel cognitive dissonance every time I go through a fast food drive-through. For starters I've been interested in eating healthy since my early 20s and I know it's important to eat fresh and unprocessed foods, preferably organic and grass-fed.

Then there's the whole multi-national thing and the less-than-likeable palm oil policies many fast food franchises ascribe to. I care what happens to the forests of Indonesia and especially what happens to those cute orangutans. When it comes to these sorts of companies, my list of issues with them is rather long.

So I feel like a traitor to the orangutans, the health industry, myself, and mankind in general when I drive through that drive-through. Yet, now and then, I still find myself ordering a thick shake.

'And, yes, thank you, I will have fries with that!'

Once I was describing cognitive dissonance at one of my workshops and a guy yelled out he had a great example. He did. He told the group about how he worked in a mine for a big corporation so he could earn enough money to build himself a straw bale house and live off the grid in order to protect the environment. He felt terrible working for a mining company yet he still continued to do it.

I knew someone who prided himself on his open, unbiased, racially-inclusive thinking yet who freaked out when his son got engaged to a woman from another culture. This is just the sort of situation that brings up that very uncomfortable feeling.

THE DISCOMFORT ZONE

Understanding more about cognitive dissonance theory has been wonderful, fabulous and enlightening because it explains:

Why we mis-remember.

Why we forget.

Why we hang on to our beliefs in the face of evidence to the contrary.

Why we don't want to hear the other side of the story.

Why we make things up.

Why we ignore vital information.

I'M A GOOD PERSON

You think of yourself as a good person, you'd have to be, heck you're reading a book on relationships. Only a good person does that. You know you're a kind person, a reasonable person. Sure you have a few quirks, and yes, there might be days you've behaved a little out of character, and it was out-of character, because you're a good person. Not lazy, not vindictive, not bad, not biased and definitely not stupid. And you're very, definitely not cruel or dishonest either.

Well so you'd like to think.

Tavris/Aronson throw a lot of light on how our brains work. I hadn't previously realised how badly my brain wants me to be right or to what extent it would go to make sure my failures are covered up or excused. I learned about 'confirmation bias' which is my brain scanning for information that confirms my belief and, conveniently, ignoring information that conflicts with what I believe. This is what all those blind spots are for.

THE SAVIOUR OF UNCOMFORTABLE FEELINGS

We all spend our lives working out what we value and creating an image of who we are. We have dearly-held stories that back this image up and we are devoted to those tales. Our self-image has been constructed by us and we will do anything to hang on to it. When we, ourselves, do something that threatens to mess with that self image, dissonance lets us know we need help.

Never fear, though, help is on the way. Your very considerate brain sends a shining saviour to ride in and snatch away that dreadful feeling. His name? Self-justification.

MY SAVIOUR, SELF-JUSTIFICATION

When you bump up against your blind spots you don't like what you see so then your brain must find a way to explain to you what is going on. Preferably an explanation that mirrors your core belief you are a nice person and you see things as they really are. Your clever brain, the one that knows you are absolutely right, will rush about and assemble plausible sounding reasons to justify whatever you said or did that has caused this sudden bout of cognitive dissonance. Your brain will do this quietly, so quietly you don't even know it's happening until you suddenly have a wonderful bit of self-justification on the tip of your tongue or running around in your mind. Your brain will always find a way to make you look good to yourself.

One of the things that stunned me when reading '*Mistakes Were Made*' was this quote, and I really want to draw a line around it because now we're getting to the heart of why things go so terribly wrong and why so many relationships don't survive.

> *'Misunderstandings, conflicts, personality differences, and even angry quarrels are not the assassins of love; self-justification is.'*

This is the biggie don't you think? Maybe read it a few times.

REMOVING INADEQUACY

A friend of mine works in a large corporate environment where self-justification is rampant. Her colleague Dan is one great example. Dan applied for a job within the corporation and was shocked to find he didn't get it. He'd been acting in the position for six months and during that time had received repeated feedback from his manager he wasn't meeting the key performance indicators. Dan's cavalier response to each warning was to tell his colleagues the boss didn't know what he was talking about and to ignore his boss's advice.

Despite his over-confident assumptions, Dan failed to get the job and instead was offered a slightly less prestigious but comparable position. Dan didn't take the news very well. He stormed out of the meeting, slammed doors on his way and accused the boss of being a bully. Not content to just badmouth the boss to everyone at the office, Dan instigated formal bullying charges against him.

Despite Dan's accusations being dismissed as untrue at every level he took them to, Dan continued to fight for almost a year until he had finally exhausted every option on offer. All the time this was happening Dan was on extended stress leave claiming he was the victim.

Dan could not deal with the idea he'd lost the job due to his own inadequacies, so he had to find a reason for what had happened. The fact the appeals' process indicated there wasn't an issue with his boss didn't penetrate his illusion. It didn't give him pause for thought. He never stopped to consider the possibility he'd been wrong. He'd been self-justifying from the beginning, shifting blame for his own poor performance to his boss's inadequacies. He was primed for further self-justification because he'd already refused so many times to see his own role in problems as they arose.

Had he listened to his boss's advice along the way and thought to himself, 'Gee I might lose this job if I don't pull my socks up', he probably wouldn't have reacted the way he did. I think this quote from Pema Chödrön gives me a glimpse into how all this works.

> *'Once you create a self-justifying storyline, your emotional entrapment within it quadruples.'*

OH MR PRESIDENT

And this is exactly the sort of thing that happened with George Bush. Many years of justifying his own behaviour, probably starting with small things, had allowed him to believe he was doing the right thing. The idea he'd made a horrific mistake wouldn't have entered his head. The lies he told were 'truths' to him. We quickly believe our own fabrications and then have trouble believing the truth could be any different.

So we have an answer to my second question from chapter three.

> Q: 'Why didn't George Bush admit he was wrong?'
>
> A: In his mind he had nothing to admit. He wasn't aware he had anything to take responsibility for.

Apparently George Bush isn't the only American President to have indulged in rampant self-justification. I also found this example in *'Mistakes Were Made'*:

> *'Lyndon Johnson was a master of self-justification. According to his biographer Robert Caro, when Johnson came to believe in something, he would believe in it "totally, with absolute conviction, regardless of previous beliefs, or of the facts in the matter." George Reedy, one of Johnson's aides, said that he "had a remarkable capacity to convince himself that he held the principles he should hold at any given time, and there was something charming about the air of injured innocence with which he would treat anyone who brought forth evidence that he had held other views in the past. It was not an act... He had a fantastic capacity to persuade himself that the 'truth' which was convenient for the present was the truth and anything that conflicted with it was the prevarication of enemies. He literally willed what was in his mind to become reality." Although Johnson's supporters found this to be a rather charming aspect of the man's character, it might well have been one of the major reasons that Johnson could not extricate the country from the quagmire of Vietnam. A president who justifies his actions only to the public might be induced to change them. A president who has justified his actions to himself, believing that he has the truth, becomes impervious to self-correction.'*

When I read, hear and see things like this, it's kinda scary don't you think? Imagine how many world leaders have operated like this. Imagine how many times you've operated like this.

It is our great big, often unconscious, preference to avoid responsibility that has us so ardently pointing the finger and blaming others.

OFFICER, OFFICER, IT WASN'T ME, IT WAS THEM

I was listening to a podcast of ABC radio's *'Conversations With Richard Fidler'* and heard Graeme Long being interviewed. Graeme is a former prison chaplain and, at the time of the interview, a pastor at The Wayside Chapel in Sydney. Graeme said something that blew me away, he said on average it takes four to five years for prisoners to begin to take responsibility for their crimes. I was staggered. Four to five years?

This Kind of blows my mind.

This is someone who has been before a jury and been found guilty. This is someone whose crime is on public record and their crime is known to their whole family. This is someone whose crime might well have appeared in the press. This is someone who is sitting in prison face-to-face with the results of their actions. This is someone who has had time to think about what they did. And yet it takes this someone four to five years to begin to truly own it.

Long said it isn't that they deny the crime. They generally don't. It's that they feel other people had roles in their actions which in some way excuses their behavior. They have a self-justifying story that might even cast the victims as those responsible.

If prisoners are reluctant to take responsibility when they're experiencing the tangible repercussions of their actions, how likely is it that you or I will admit to what we've done? If these same prisoners are still pretty sure, after years in prison, that the real culprits are walking around free outside the prison, how likely is it that you and I will blame someone else?

I'D JUST LIKE TO POINT OUT

I've suffered under the delusion (and I'm very embarrassed to admit this publicly) that people would really like to know when they had a problem because I thought if I told them about it then they'd have a less problematic life.

As I said, embarrassing, what sort of idiot does this?

As I've started to see the capabilities I have for self-delusion, it has, rather wonderfully, explained more clearly why I've had some very cold and defensive responses to my helpful 'pointing out' of the sins of others.

People don't like their self-justifying shit shaken up! I've learned to be much more in control of my very 'helpful' tendencies.

REASONS FOR THEIR RACISM

In a study, published by Edward Jones and Rika Kohler in The Journal of Abnormal and Social Psychology in 1958, the researchers uncovered something interesting about memory when they visited a Southern town in USA.

This was the late 1950s and, especially in the South, there were strong opinions on both sides of the racial divide. It was a very hot topic. Jones and Kohler selected people with very strong opinions from both sides of the divide, then presented them with a set of arguments for both views. So all participants, no matter their views, were reading arguments that supported both their own stances and also the stances of the other side. The arguments they were shown were a mixed bag, some were just ridiculous and others were quite sound and reasoned.

Afterwards the researchers found both sides easily recalled the plausible arguments in favour of their position but forgot the arguments that favoured their position if the argument was silly.

And the opposite was also found and both sides could easily recall the silly arguments supporting the views they were vehemently against. Completely unconsciously these individuals had only taken in what suited their beliefs, unless it was evidence that further enhanced their stands by making the alternative views ridiculous.

Why did this happen? Great question. I'll tell you all about it in the next chapter.

INCOMING LIGHT

It's easy to see.

All this makes sense once it's been pointed out. If you can really get a handle on what self-justification is, you can improve every single relationship you have because you won't be as likely to get stuck in the blame game and you won't employ 'the assassin of love' so frequently.

Of course you'll still have blind spots. Of course you'll still self justify. Just knowing about this or even looking reflectively inside for the truth won't change how your brain works. It's always in protective mode.

However, awareness of your vulnerabilities in this area may mean you find your blind spots are letting in a little more light.

For me, and I believe this is true for most of us, I see one huge part of myself in frantic motion to cover up, blame and run away from dissonance-causing behaviour. And when I stop and examine this urge, I can see another part of me craving the freedom of transparency, desiring to be brave and wanting to take responsibility. I believe this is the deeper part of me and this is where peace and joy is found. Tarvis/Aronson frame it beautifully:

> *'Courageous individuals take us straight into the heart of dissonance and its innermost irony: The mind wants to protect itself from the pain of dissonance with the balm of self-justification and the soul wants to confess.'*

Let us be courageous individuals.

Something I really love about humanity, about how you and I are constructed, is how fabulously we do when people apologise to us. I love that rush of mercy and goodwill I feel when someone genuinely says 'sorry'. One minute I am up-in-arms furious and the next I want to comfort my 'enemy'. Receiving the same from others is to receive grace, and the effect of grace is healing, bonding and feels just plain wonderful.

When I face my fears and take responsibility I gain two incredible things; self-respect and the opportunity to be known for who I am. To be known for who I am and loved regardless is surely on par with the best of miracles.

PRACTICE

Run Toward Confession

When our mistake, sin or failure is exposed we have to choose if we're going to make a run toward confession or if we are going to continue to cover up, blame and justify. One will heal you, grow love and make you strong.

I like this quote by Gandhi:

'Confession of errors is like a broom which sweeps away the dirt and leaves the surface brighter and cleaner. I feel stronger after confession.'

You have a choice.

Choose bravery, choose relationships, choose love.

'Time
and memory
are true artists;
they remould reality
nearer to the
heart's desire.'

JOHN DEWEY

6

THE SELF-SERVING HISTORIAN

At the end of the previous chapter I told you about the racial divide rivals and their recall of the various arguments they were given to read. Both sides remembered only the arguments that suited their beliefs and immediately forgot arguments that might have challenged their way of thinking.

There's a very good reason this happened. Memory was at work.

The favourite weapon of the saviour of uncomfortable feelings – self-justification – is memory.

In this chapter I'll be exploring some of what I've learned about memory. I find this is a completely fascinating topic though I came to be interested in memory originally because I was interested in finding out how to handle stress.

One of the world's leading researchers on stress is Rockefeller University's Prof Bruce McEwan. I came across his work when I was looking into the effect of stress on my brain. I've read some of his research and one quote in particular stood out.

'Most of our psychological stress is from our past.'

Following up on the implications of this quote, eventually opened me up to some different ways of handling stress and a new take on memory. If my past was the cause of much of my emotional pain and stress, then I needed to know more about memory.

What McEwan pointed out made sense. I did spend a lot of time going over and over what had happened in the past. I thought constantly about what so and so had said; what so and so had done; what tone they'd said it in; what I had done; what I hadn't done; what I thought they thought; what I thought they thought about what they thought I thought; and ever more ridiculous circles that were endless and worrying.

Gaining more understanding about my memory has been a 'get out of jail free card', as far as stressing about what happened in the past.

THE MEMORABLE MEMORY

Some helpful things to know about the memory are:

Recent memories are more readily accessed. Basically your brain is busy and doesn't have time to take the back stairs to the attic and hang around sorting through cobwebs and crap to find your old memories, when it can clearly see something that happened just yesterday sitting right here on the desk. Your brain loves an easy option.

Emotional situations are easier for your brain to recall. This is pretty self-explanatory. The stuff that makes a big emotional impact makes a bigger impression on your brain. Easy.

You re-live your memories. This is something you're well familiar with. You've experienced the rush of adrenalin when you recall the scary situation. You've felt grief flood your body with chemicals when you recall the death of someone close to you. We don't need to be experiencing a situation in current time to experience the physiological/emotional effects of it.

Memories take years to form. Okay, so now I'm getting into territory that surprised me. Years to form? Hang on, isn't my brain just taking snaps of my life and storing them neatly and immediately, in files for me to grab when I need them?

The answer here is 'apparently not'.

This is, again, material from 'Brain Rules' by John Medina and the bad news is that, just like sight, your memories are open to interpretation. They won't be a true record of what has happened to you and they form slowly over years. In the time they're forming, prior to consolidation, they're especially vulnerable to change.

You decide your memories. What you say, who you talk to, how you spin the situation, what you tell people about what happened and many other things, will contribute to what that memory actually ends up being.

Yes, it's you. You are creating the story inside your head that is the past.

I know! Drat.

Here you were thinking you had lots of factual evidence safely recorded in your head when it's actually all open to interpretation, change, and can even be pure fantasy. This might be especially disappointing news if you've carried a nice righteous grudge for a long time.

I'd created some fabulous stories about some members of the film festival board. In my mind they'd become a coven of evil witches bent on destroying me through their underhand ways. This is a very useful story for me. However, it doesn't have anything to do with truth because I've created motives for them that are just that: created.

I don't know what their motives were. I don't know why it happened. Were they worried that big names coming on the board might mean a loss of power for them? Or was it as my board member 'friend' had said? Had this been solely a big favour to me? I don't know their motives but I do know the long, the crazy hours were damaging my health. I do know if I hadn't been 'encouraged' to leave, I wouldn't have discovered all the amazing things I've since learned.

And I'd never have been living near the beach as I am now. As the Festival Patron, Aussie actor, Tony Barry so beautifully put it, 'Don't worry Toni, this is a gift in shitty wrapping paper'. So I actually have a lot to thank those board members for. As with most of our life-disasters, it takes a while to see their real value.

Recent and somewhat controversial research by researcher Karim Nader from New York University suggests the very act of recalling a memory changes it and memories are vulnerable all the time, not just in the years when they are forming.

It would appear that memories are much more fragmentary than we've previously thought and aren't even stored nice and neatly in just one place in the brain. When assembling a memory your brain will take information from a variety of places.

The very real possibility with all the sad and bad stories we tell about our tragedies, is we can exaggerate or minimise parts of the stories when we tell them. Then the next time we tell the story we can easily think the parts we changed are actually true.

LET'S GO TO A CONCERT

Here's a little scenario to get you thinking.

Close your eyes and imagine you're in a concert hall, one that has fine acoustics. You're sitting in the best seats in the house, the place you'd most want to be, and your favourite band, let's call them Wonderful, is walking onto the stage. You're very excited, you've waited so long for this concert and you went to loads of trouble to get these seats. Wonderful begins, you breathe out, and sink into bliss. Finally you're in the moment you've been waiting for.

Tip: Close your eyes after you finish reading the instructions rather than when I say close your eyes.

The concert is great, the acoustics incredible and they're singing better than you've ever heard them sing. There's an unexpected special moment when another of your favourite singers comes onto the stage and performs with the lead singer. What a delicious surprise. It's an incredible concert and you feel like the luckiest person in the world.

Throughout the evening the band perform all of your favourite songs. This night is unsurpassed among your concert experiences. You're feeling elated when, almost at the end of the night, the man to your left leans across and vomits in your lap. You can open your eyes.

WHAT'S YOUR STORY?

Now you have a story to tell, and you'll start telling it straight away. Will you post pictures of the band on Instagram and rave about the evening? Will you call your friends and tell them the horrific news someone vomited in your lap. Will you

Instagram the vomit? How will you tell the story to your mum, your boss, your colleagues? What have others who attended the concert said? Did they point out things you'd missed? What did they post on Facebook about it? What was your comment? In two months are you still telling the same story you started with? Chances are the story has changed.

Your memories will evolve and these things will be some of the influences on the memory you form:

What you tell others.

How you tell others.

The tone of your voice.

The tone of their response.

What others say.

What those who were with you say happened.

What you hear in the news.

What you post online.

What response you get to what you post online.

And on, and on. In time you'll form a memory of that night. The 'truth' about what happened. You know your memory is true, you were there and you saw it with your own eyes.

FIVE YEARS FROM NOW

Five years on from that night you might tell of the incredible evening when Wonderful sang and you'll share the joy you experienced. Or five years on, you might talk about how horrible it was to get vomited on at a great concert.

Or five years from that night, you might be telling the story of the unbelievable evening when there was an outbreak of illness at a concert. You can't quite recall which concert you were at, though you do remember the moment people began vomiting — vomit was everywhere! The concert was cancelled it was so bad.

While I was writing this book I was talking to a friend about memory. She was excited to tell me what had happened when she'd visited her mother the day before. She'd said to her mum, 'Remember when we were living at Harbord and had to climb all those stairs up from the beach?' Her mother replied 'We never lived at Harbord'. Moments later my friend's uncle arrived and she sought confirmation of her memory by asking him about it 'Do you remember living at Harbord?' He smiled at the memory and replied 'Oh yes, that place with all those stairs to the beach'. Despite what her uncle said her mother still insisted they never lived at Harbord. She's not quite sure how to handle her mum denying what she knows to be true.

THE SELF-SERVING HISTORIAN

As I mentioned earlier in this chapter, I'd already developed an interest in memory and I was especially curious about the disparity between the stories I'd heard, not only around the film festival debacle, but other subsequent problems I'd experienced with fellow humans. Who was right? Which story was true? None of them were remotely close to my story. So just who was lying?

I've come to understand that in all liklihood no one was deliberately lying.

Only days before my meeting with Very Nice I'd been avidly reading, for the first time, the *'Mistakes Were Made'* book and it was making a huge impression. As you've heard, this book explains why it is humans are prone to dismiss, ignore or forget information that makes them look bad.

When Very Nice was telling me about what had just happened to her, I was reminded of what I'd just read, so I was anxious to put their findings to the test. Could this stuff be possible? Could someone like Very Nice be forgetting to include parts of the story that reflected badly on her?

To tell you the truth I didn't really expect Very Nice's answer.

Yes, she could. She'd entirely neglected one key part – her role! What was very interesting to me was how quickly she'd forgotten. It took me asking the question to prompt her memory and, even then, it wasn't immediate recall. She looked surprised when she remembered, then horrified when the full memory of her actions hit her. Yet Cruella had yelled at her only an hour or so before she'd told me the story.

I'm really curious to know if she would have remembered her role at all if I'd asked her three weeks after the event and after she'd already told the story multiple times. And here comes another life-changing quote from '*Mistakes Were Made*' and these words inspired my chapter title.

'Memory becomes our personal live in, self-serving historian.'

USEFUL FOOT SOLDIERS

So not only is our memory being rather selective when it comes to our role in something uncomfortable, it also employs some less-than-nice workers to get the job done. Tavris/Aronson put it delightfully:

'Confabulation, distortion and just plain forgetting are the foot soldiers of memory.'

Apparently, without even thinking about it, or planning it, you'll put these foot soldiers to work when you do something that causes you to feel shame, embarrassment or discomfort, especially if what happened is at odds with the way you like to think about yourself.

Don't worry though, it's not just you. It's all of us and we do this, for the most part, unconsciously.

Scary huh?

BUT I DO THE HOUSEWORK!

Apparently your brain will always calculate everything in your favour. It might well exaggerate how many athletic medals you were awarded, how far you walked on a hike or who your friends were at school. In business ventures it's common for one partner to feel the other partners have the better deal. Interestingly, the other partners are thinking exactly the same thing.

Tavris/Aronson mention studies where husbands and wives are asked to calculate how much housework they do, and this inspired me to ask the same question in my workshops.

I ask the women to yell out how much they do. It's usually high, between 70-90% unless they have a cleaner, then they yell small numbers and make everyone else jealous. Then I ask the guys to tell me what the real situation is. They yell out a much broader range of 30-60%. Then everyone has a good laugh because it's clear someone is over-estimating (though not them of course).

I've observed the same in myself. I'm usually pretty sure I did more work than others on a project and my role was more key to the outcome. We're likely to underestimate details about failed exams, silly mistakes and relationship failures if we feel those things might not reflect well on us. Tavris/Aronson again:

'If mistakes were made memory helps us remember that they were made by someone else. If we were there, we were just innocent bystanders.'

The dark side of this is we'll minimise our mistakes while maximising the mistakes of others.

And we run straight to blame in order to deflect attention from anything we might have done.

HOW COULD THEY?

Your brain doesn't easily notice what you are doing to others. It can, however, definitely feel the incredible amount of pain 'they' inflicted on you. If your friend is cruel to you you'll wonder how they could possibly have behaved like that. It's incomprehensible to you.

Between both 'catastrophes', and life in general, my mind was bursting with, 'How could they? How could they hurt me so terribly? How come it didn't bother them?'. And those questions brought their own friends along like, 'What sort of people are they?' I was confused that people I knew could suddenly behave in a way that seemed to me to be casually cruel.

The relief I felt on finding out about blind spots, naive realism, self-justification and memory was huge because then I understood more fully how blind we all are to the pain we cause others. When people hurt us it doesn't mean there now was any intentional cruelty involved.

It seems we are mostly unable to fathom the way we, ourselves, affect other people. This also made me realise that, while I'd been brilliant at magnifying the pain they'd caused me, I didn't have a good understanding of how I might have hurt or distressed them. Through reading *'Mistakes Were Made'* I came to understand this:

> When my brain calculates in my favour, one of the side effects is that I fail to understand the level of pain I have inflicted on someone else.

Very sobering don't you think?

When someone hurts you, you're likely to attribute all sorts of motives to them. You'll come up with rational reasons why this has happened, exaggerate their intent and also wind up the magnitude of the pain they've caused. You're likely to feel, strongly (especially if they're friends or family), that you wouldn't behave in a similar manner, so they must be the ones who are abnormal. Too something! All of this will strengthen your blame stance.

Of course it is also true some people are aware they're causing you pain and just don't care. However I don't think this is the case with most people.

NOT SO VERY NICE

So we've come to another answer for one of the questions from chapter three.

Q: 'Why didn't Cruella apologise to Very Nice?'

A: Because Cruella doesn't feel like she did anything wrong.

In Cruella's mind Very Nice is to blame. Very Nice started it. In fact, Cruella doesn't think Very Nice is very nice. She thinks she's mean, aggressive and, exactly what she'd already announced to the office, controlling.

If Cruella had any niggles of conscience about her outburst, she'll have quickly self-justified. Cruella probably told herself her outburst was a reasonable and protective response to an attack and therefore Very Nice deserved everything she got. She'd smoothed things out as Tavris/Aronson explain:

> *'At the simplest level, memory smoothes out the wrinkles of dissonance by enabling the confirmation bias to hum along, selectively causing us to forget discrepant, disconfirming information about beliefs we hold dear.'*

Very Nice told me when she apologised to Cruella, Cruella was quite haughty towards her and had a 'Well! It's about time' entitled sort of attitude to Very Nice's apology. Very Nice didn't get any sense Cruella thought there was anything she needed to say sorry for.

THE EVER HANDY PARENTS

The great thing about parents, and probably teachers too, is they're terribly handy for a good bit of blame-shifting, as no one can really check the facts. Your friends, acquaintances and co-workers weren't around. You can say what you like and embellish without fear of being found out. Parents are safely in the distance. You know mistakes were made and with this handy pair standing off-stage right, it's quick and easy to point to the real source of the problem. A source that is, conveniently, not you. As Tavris/Aronson point out, you'd like any flaws in you to be easily explained by the mistakes made by *them.*

> *'Parent blaming is a popular and convenient form of self-justification because it allows people to live less uncomfortably with their regrets and imperfections.'*

What's really been a big surprise for me was to find out these memories, the things I point to as explanations for me, these stories about my life I hold as sacred, aren't static and solid. They change. So not only don't I remember them accurately to begin with, my memories are changeable depending on my current relationship with the people in my life.

Kind of mind-boggling when you really think about it.

Tavris/Aronson explain if we have a good current relationship with our parents then our brains will recall positive memories of our time with them and our childhoods. Apparently we'll spin them 'up' to make them even more delightful and the reverse is also true. When we have difficult relationships with our parents, then our brains will deliver more negative memories. These might well be an exaggerated version of how tough our childhood was or how awful our parents were.

> Q: 'Why are the teenagers remembering the same conflict so differently?'
>
> A: Because current relationship-status affects memory recall.

Also surprising to note in the Feeney/Cassidy research, mentioned in chapter three, how little time had passed before the kids 'mis-remembered' the events. It was only six weeks between interviews. Also, in the case of this particular experiment, the kids had to articulate and write down their answers both times. They got to really think about what they were saying and yet still came up with different memories, different answers.

Those kids thought they were telling the truth both times. No one is lying. They're telling the story as they remember it and it's true to them.

THE BRILLIANT DECEIVERS

How much more vulnerable are you or I to telling skewed versions of childhood events or having exaggerated judgements of our parents when nothing we say is being recorded and we're telling various versions to a whole range of people?

Everything I've read on this subject would tell me that I'm very vulnerable.

If I add the passage of time and input from other people, and throw in my own emotional state from day-to-day, then I can see my tales about my parents could well be fantasy. My tales about my teachers, my childhood and, hey, anything that happened longer than six weeks ago, could well be littered with lies, false memories, mis-remembering and biased-takes. Six weeks? Try six minutes or even six seconds.

Down the track I asked Very Nice how long she though it took to forget her role in the conflict. 'Instantly,' she replied.

She'd wiped her role in the conflict from her mind straight away and reacted with outrage at Cruella's actions immediately.

ME AND MY MUM

This brings me back to the story in chapter two about when Phil and I were getting married. I talked about something my mum had said, something I've been telling people for almost 40 years. However, it's a story my mum has only just read while being part of the editing team for this book and she thinks I've made it up.

She's 86, sharp as a tack and doing a great job.

My story is that my mum said, 'He's too good for you'. Have I made it up? We'll never know. Off the top of my head I can come up with a few possible explanations.

I made it up: I love a good bit of drama and a great story. Hell, I tell stories for a living. It's a very dramatic line and evokes a shocked response, 'Her mother said that? Toni must have been truly awful'. Everyone's intrigued. Now I speak about relationships, any dramatic relationship stories I happen to come across are gold. However if I made it up, then why was I telling Phil about it the same day it happened? Could I have been playing a little victim role? Quite possibly. Could I have been after sympathy and playing a 'mean mother' card? Quite possibly.

I altered it: This could well be the true one. Mum said something and, immediately, I took her to mean she thought Phil was too good for me. This explanation fits in well to the self-pitying way I looked at life then. I find this sort of 'mis-hearing' happens all the time. I'm always amused when, after my workshops, people tell me what particular thing I've said has spoken to them. At least half the time they're things I haven't said. They're things they've heard. Even during the workshops, when people get up to talk about something I've just been speaking about, I'm fascinated by how much of what I said has already altered. In minutes!

Mum's totally forgotten: Contrary to popular opinion our brains don't remember everything, our brains discard most of what happens. Comments we make, things we do, places we go, people we meet, are simply wiped clean from our memory unless our brain decides they are important. This comment, if it happened at all, was made nearly 40 years ago and may not have been any more than a quick throwaway line while mum was in the middle of doing something else. Flying a plane for instance She had her pilot's license, parachuted and ran a variety of businesses. If this is the case, then she probably barely registered the comment and hasn't thought of it since, so it's unlikely to be in her memory bank.

My mum's never been average.

Mum's self-serving historian is at work: When mum and I discussed our misaligned memories, her argument was 'It's totally unlike me to say something like that'. She reminded me how supportive she'd been at the time (and she had, very), so she's very sure she would never have said something so harsh. It would have been out of character. Aha! When is it that self-justification and memory come riding in? When we've behaved in contrast to our dearly-held self-image.

Of course my original story could also be true. You choose the one you like. I'm sticking to my story, though I'm pretty open to the second option as well. Whichever you choose to believe, I do want you to know I have a great mum and she isn't someone who'd set out to be deliberately mean.

Writing this just reminded me of an embarrassing instance to do with having zero recall of a situation that actually happened. We were introduced to a couple some years ago who said they already knew us from years before.

We asked them to remind us about the meeting. 'Meeting? We were friends. We came to your house for Christmas!' Try as I might I couldn't recall ever having met them, so I couldn't pull off the,'Oh, yes, silly me. I remember!' It was very awkward. Phil managed to scrape up a few memories, but I've never been able to recall ever having met them. They didn't look even vaguely familiar and yet they came for Christmas! I've met them many times since, they live nearby, and I still search their faces for clues and come up with nothing. Weird.

You and I, we're brilliant deceivers and accomplished at believing our own lies, a subject I'll keep exploring in the next chapter. I'll also talk about some of the ways we can do better at keeping our self-justifying tendencies at bay.

PRACTICE

Remember You Don't Remember

Rather than leaping to blame others keep in mind that your memory is fragile, you're dreadfully biased to your side of the story and you have whopping blind spots.

Get a little less attached to seeing others as the problem.

'One of the best
ways to make yourself
happy is to make other people
happy. One of the best ways
to make other people happy
is to be happy
yourself.'

GRETCHEN RUBIN

THE HAPPINESS PROJECT

7

THE HAPPINESS CONNECTION

As you've seen in the past few chapters, humans are more than a little self-deceptive. The lies we tell may be unintentional and the dissembling will usually go unrecognised by ourselves. However neither of these things alter the end result: We have a firm belief in our own fallacies.

People can become so convinced of the truth of their own story that sometimes they even go to court and fight a legal battle regarding their version of events. Which brings me back to Sarah, you'll remember her from the chapter on questions, she's the one who left her family for a nice, shiny, younger man.

IN ORDER TO LIVE WITH HERSELF

As I mentioned, Sarah brought 14 lawsuits against Paul in eight years. What on earth was she thinking? Well we can't really know for certain though I'm going to give you the explanation I think is a likely one.

Knowing this family well, and knowing Sarah, I'd be willing to bet she was incredibly, even squirmingly, uncomfortable with her decision. The cognitive dissonance alarm bells weren't just ringing, they were clanging. Her actions were in such direct contrast to her long-held values and beliefs it's likely that friends and family weren't the only ones shocked. I suspect Sarah was also shocked by the enormity of what she had done.

When it came down to it she was left with two choices:

> **One:** Own up to what would have been, according to her Christian beliefs, selfish and immoral behaviour.
>
> **Two:** Quickly come up with a jolly good explanation that would deflect the blame away from her.

Sarah believes she's a nice person, an honest person, and very definitely a good mother. Good mothers don't just leave their children for no real reason. She's been raised to believe that marriage is forever. Honest, good people don't walk out on good husbands or cheat on them. Sarah couldn't live with option number one, so she needed a real reason and a bad husband to make sense of what she'd done. Choice two allows her to live with herself.

> Q: 'Why is Sarah attacking him for her decision?'
>
> A: Someone has to be to blame and it cannot be her.

When we self-justify, we come to believe our own excuses and Sarah likely came to believe her own story so completely, the lawsuits were a no-brainer. She's a good person. She'll fight for what is right and for what is rightfully hers. Sarah feels little or no guilt. Sarah has no need to apologise or take responsibility because self-justification, blind spots, naive realism and her memory have reorganised the facts. In fact Sarah probably feels Paul deserves a little pain after all the terrible pain he caused her. Of course he does! Because of him her family is forever shattered. The explanation is, according to '*Mistakes Were Made*':

'We mis-remember in order to live with ourselves.'

SO WHAT TO DO NOW?

Excellent question. And my answer is, become aware of, and

reduce, the amount you self-justify. You don't want to damage precious relationships with self-justification, and there are other knock-on effects you'll want to avoid such as:

Inability to learn from mistakes: When you self-justify you don't see your role and therefore you don't see where you went wrong. You are doomed to repeat your behaviour.

Prone to making poor decisions: Having a good handle on what is really happening allows you to make wise decisions. When you self-justify you distort reality and won't be as likely to make the smarter decisions.

Falling deeper into the hole: One self-justification leads to another, and then another and next thing you're in a very deep hole. This is how George Bush ended up in a war that wasn't warranted. The more you push your excuses and blame others, the less able you are to see clearly and understand what is right and wrong. You are in a deep hole that obliterates your ability to see.

Little problems turn into big ones: In the effort to push the blame from yourself, you are prone to overplaying the issues and exaggerating the role of the other party. They come back at you with their own self-justification and next thing is you have big problems, when a little humility to begin with could have sorted the little problem easily.

A FEW IDEAS

So just a few ideas to get you started:

Feel It: To start, you are going to have to learn to take note of that cognitive dissonance. Stop and feel it, tune in. Once you start noticing it you'll be in a place where you can see your vulnerability in that situation. So start there.

Empathy It: Start with empathy rather than defence. This is a person not an enemy. They, too, are prone to bewildering blind spots, naive realism and self-justification. Treat them gently. They're as fragile as you and they likely mean you no harm.

Accept It: Accept you make mistakes, can be irrational, might well have been rude or thoughtless. It's not the end of the world. You are no better, and likely no worse, than the rest of us mortals trying to make sense of living on Earth. Put your sword, your shield and your fear down. Tavris/Aronson advise:

> *'Learn to see mistakes not as terrible personal failings to be denied or justified but as inevitable aspects of life that help us grow, and grow up.'*

Admit It: If you're feeling dissonance, then listen to the message. Something is amiss. As I mentioned in one of the Practices earlier, you may need to run to confession.

One of the very strongest aspects to our marriage is that Phil and I have learned to relate with a minimum of self-defence. I admit my stuff. He admits his. Then we have fun making up.

If we want our relationship to survive we have to put our empathy for one another ahead of our desire to defend. Strong partnerships, marriages and friendships are built on vulnerability and openness, built on the admission, 'Yes, I behaved like a prick. I'm sorry'.

The next bit may seem, for a while, as if I've lost the plot. I haven't, I'm going to wind back to a really important way you can cut down your self-justification.

AND UNDERNEATH ALL THAT?

Have you ever thought maybe the reason, even a very big reason, some of your relationships haven't worked is that you still believe in fairytales? The myth, the story, the fantasy that someone else will make you happy? I think we're all, at least unconsciously, addicted to fairytales and happily ever-after happy.

For the most part, movies have happy endings. Yet most marriages don't. We often measure our parents, siblings, grandparents, children and our own lives by fictional film and television depictions of what a family should be. Yet most families are nothing like the TV ones.

Through media, television, movies, school, families and social media, we develop ideas about what success is; what careers we'll have; what a good job is; how friends behave and what it takes to be happy. Then we chase those things with all our might.

Most of it is bullshit and most of it leaves us feeling let down, as though we've missed out on 'real' life and somehow managed to get the leftovers. Please don't email me and tell me about all the exceptions to my generalisations, I know. This is a book. I'm making a point.

One needs a little drama in a book.

I HAVE VERY BAD NEWS FOR YOU

None of that stuff will make you happy.

Prince Charming or Snow White are not coming to save you. You didn't buy the right ticket in the lottery. The job you long for is unlikely to meet your expectations. Your new Smartphone will be dated in no time at all. And the travels will end.

Most of what we 'get' in the pursuit of happiness is transitory and doesn't deliver what we hoped for. Your husband, wife, child, mother, father, boss, friend or long-lost uncle will not make you happy. Momentarily yes, they may amuse, delight and bring you much joy. However they cannot deliver happiness to you long-term.

Nonetheless we continue to expect others to deliver happiness and get frustrated when they don't.

Not only that, your expectation that others need to pull their socks up, get their act together or change so you can be happy, is a pretty good way to ensure you remain unhappy.

It's ridiculous when you think about it. I make myself angry and unhappy because some poor soul, who never promised to make me happy, won't change their behaviour in order to make me happy.

SOMETIMES RELATIONSHIPS END

I don't expect all relationships to have a happy ending. Relationships end – it's what prompted me to write this book. Sometimes a relationship ending, such as when there is abuse, is the best possible outcome for you.

Sometimes relationships end because it's one that just didn't work out. You may have rushed into a friendship or marriage without really getting to know the person. You might work for a narcissist. Your mother-in-law might be someone so negative you cannot be around her. There is any mix of possibilities where, no matter how hard you try, it ends.

Apologies to all mother-in-laws, I don't mean you. My own mother-in-law is great.

Sometimes relationships end because you were in bed or in business with the wrong people. George Vaillant, author of '*Triumphs of Experience*', the book I mentioned in chapter one, observed some of the men involved in the study who had divorced a few times went on to have long-lived and very happy marriages on a third or fourth try.

Sometimes relationships end because you each value the relationship differently. You can't sort out your problems with everyone. You might be the only one interested in resolving the conflict. Unless you want to be a bully, you can't force people to talk things through, discuss the problem, find resolution or be interested in both sides of the story.

Sometimes relationships end because they've served their purpose. An interviewer once asked cultural anthropologist Margaret Mead to what she attributed the failure of her three marriages. 'I don't know what you mean,' she said, 'I had three very successful marriages, all for different developmental phases of my life'. So with that out on the table, hopefully I've made it clear I'm not talking about all relationships in this next paragraph.

HE DOESN'T MAKE ME HAPPY

I was speaking at a conference recently and I'd spoken on relationships which is always a great conversation starter. People are especially intrigued to discover I didn't love Phil when we tied the knot and yet ended up with a happy marriage, so this is a topic that comes up a lot. One woman sat down next to me at lunch and told me she'd been married a long time and it wasn't going well. He loved her and, while she liked him, she didn't really love him. She'd lived apart from him on a few occasions, even living with another man for years. She said she didn't know what was wrong but that she was unhappy with him.

Interestingly, she was also a speaker on happiness.

She asked me if I had any wisdom for her. I replied, 'You know the answer'. She kept insisting she didn't and I kept saying the same sentence again and again. Eventually her eyes widened. 'I'm expecting him to make me happy?' I nodded, almost laughing that it had taken her so long.

I do exactly this myself, we're so blind to our own stuff. We really need each other.

She kept saying things like, 'That's it! That's it! He can't make me happy. What was I thinking?'

This woman was gorgeous on so many levels and a teacher on happiness and yet was making a mistake so common that almost all of us fall into it daily. She was searching for happiness outside herself and, unconsciously, burdening her husband with a job only she can do.

HERE'S WHAT I THINK WAS GOING ON

Okay, we're here now. I'm linking back to the beginning of this chapter. I imagine underneath everything that happened, the deep cause of Sarah and Paul's marriage breakdown was this:

Paul wasn't making Sarah happy. Sarah was making the mistake of looking for happiness outside herself. She'd once imagined she'd find it in her husband and kids. As happiness wasn't turning up in her living room, she opened the front door and looked outside. Sarah saw something bright and new, something tempting, something she hoped might offer her the happiness that was eluding her. So she walked out the door and shut it firmly behind her. Sadly that which was bright and new hasn't made her happy either.

Sometimes relationships end because the other person doesn't make you happy. This is the sort of ending that doesn't have to happen because this ending isn't necessarily necessary.

HAPPINESS

My big fat relationship advice? Learn how to be happy.

This might be the very reason we all have such a drive to seek happiness. Happiness is so much more profound and productive than I'd imagined. And happiness absolutely ties into ways to reduce self-justification.

When you look to people to fulfill you, it's very easy to respond with resentment at their failure to do so. You haven't yet realised you've asked the impossible.

When you're resentful, it's very hard to find joy, and very easy to find faults. This isn't a great mix and you know exactly where this will lead if it continues. Excuses, excuses, blame, blame and a whole stack of self-justification.

So this is why happiness is an important connection. Your ability to enjoy a relationship will be hugely influenced by your ability to bring happiness to the relationship. The fairytale ending isn't that someone else made you happy.

Those 'fairytales' often end in recriminations, lawsuits, and misery.

The fairytale ending is when you bring joy into the life of another person. And they bring it to you. It's the way of the Magician because it creates magic.

We'll get more into the way of the Magician in a later chapter.

Doesn't this just make sense? It's so simple it's easy to miss.

Happy people make happy relationships.

Work on your own happiness and your relationships will be happier.

When you are happier, you are naturally less defensive, kinder, more appreciative, easier to get on with, more generous, more positive and much less inclined to find fault. Happiness calms your brain, making you less likely to attack. Happiness relaxes you and, as a cool chilled relaxed person, you're less likely to interpret the comment someone made as offensive.

When you're happier, you are so much easier to be around and your happiness is contagious so those around you are more likely to be happier too. When you're happy you're not walking on to the very thin ice of demanding those around you make you happy.

Are you starting to see the connection?

The woman I had lunch with, left the table very excited about the future of her relationship with her husband once she realised that he couldn't make her happy. It's ironic isn't it? There's another piece of irony waiting for you in the next chapter and it's all about the brain. You'd think our very own brains would want to make us happy, right? Hmm, maybe not. Coming up we'll be visting Downton Abbey and finding out why we're so defensive and why we can overreact.

PRACTICE

Learn to be happier

Make learning to create your own happiness your mission for the next 12 months. Hint: The last chapter of this book is all about one of the main components.

If you get stuck you can always check out my website, there'll be plenty of resources there.

‘A very
careful watchdog
seems to be exactly what nature
has installed in our
brains to protect
us from threat and
danger.’

PROFESSOR SABINE WINDMANN

8

UPSTAIRS/DOWNSTAIRS

Sometimes, especially when there were three, four or five kids in the house, I'd completely lose it. One minute I'd be berating the kids for not cleaning up their rooms, and the next minute some she-monster would emerge and I'd be yelling and throwing out their toys. Not pretty, and really scary for my kids.

No-one was fond of the she-monster and it was hard to reconcile myself with her. For years, just when I thought I was getting my act together and becoming the oasis of calm I was aiming to be, out she'd jump and freak me out, along with everyone around me. When she was in control I wouldn't recognise myself. I'd do things I'd regret and it was, even as it was happening, as if I was watching someone else. I felt like there were two of me, one dark and one light. As it turned out, I wasn't too far off the mark.

Some years ago I read '*The Whole Brain Child*' by Dr Dan Siegel and learned there are two parts of my brain vying for control. Dr Dan helpfully dubs these areas Upstairs Brain and Downstairs Brain and these next two chapters are courtesy of the helpful wisdom in this wonderful book.

These two parts of your brain have a huge impact in your day-to-day life and massive implications for all your relationships. When it comes to your emotional life, understanding the

Upstairs Brain and Downstairs Brain is very useful, especially if you'd prefer not to find yourself face-to-face with any you-monsters. I'm more likely to either calm down quickly or stay in control during tough situations, now that I know what's happening inside my brain.

THE UPSTAIRS BRAIN

The Upstairs Brain, or cerebral cortex, is your higher function area where you make decisions, process language, perceive and do your thinking. This is where you consider options, sort and process most of your information and feel sensation. It appears long-term memory also lives here as well as your intellect, morality, intuition and personality. Yeah, Upstairs is a somewhat important area.

It's the more recently evolved part of your brain and therefore quite sophisticated. Think of it as the 'going out brain'. It knows how to dress appropriately, say the right thing and behave itself in accordance with social norms. Upstairs is also the brake and accelerator for your reactions and can help you calm fear. And it's especially important to how you do relationships:

This part of your brain lets you tune into what someone else is saying, be compassionate, have empathy and houses your capacity for self-understanding.

Obviously, you want to make sure you don't go anywhere or do anything without this bit of your brain engaged. Imagine!

THE DOWNSTAIRS BRAIN

The Downstairs Brain, or limbic system, is the area of your brain particularly devoted to keeping you alive. This is your

Downstairs Brain's most important job because if it doesn't do this job well, and you happen to die, then all the other jobs your brain had to do suddenly become redundant. It's your very own faithful watchdog and is on constant alert for anything that might be a danger to you.

The Downstairs Brain houses your motivation and many of your emotions, most especially those to do with survival and pleasure, such as fear, anger, lust and the desire for food. A lot of your emotional life starts right here.

Your basic functions such as breathing and blinking are controlled by Downstairs, as are your flight, fight and freeze responses. Downstairs is thought to be a more primitive part of the brain, very chemically reactive and always on alert. This is the instinctual and urge part of you. The urge to have a wine, chocolate or the urge for sex is your limbic system speaking up. It's just as well it does speak up or you may forget to eat.

When you're feeling very stressed, excessively emotional or you do something stupid that's against your better judgment (hey, was that Upstairs speaking?), you can bet you're operating in Downstairs mode. If you've ever done something completely mortifying, like dancing naked on a table at your office party, you can put at least some of the blame on Downstairs because Downstairs often gets you into trouble.

I'm well acquainted with mortifying.

DOWN AT DOWNTON ABBEY

I was watching Downton Abbey at the time I was reading Dan's book. A rather lovely coincidence as it turned out. There were some commonalities between the book and the household depicted in the show that became helpful visual reminders of how my brain worked.

I began to imagine the Upstairs Brain being the upstairs folk in the household. They dress to impress, make all the important decisions and hand out instructions to the obedient folk downstairs. When there's a problem they find a solution and they almost never run around screaming, get very flustered or do anything too far out of the ordinary. When they're in charge things run like clockwork.

Just like our Downstairs Brain the downstairs folk at Downton make sure everyone eats. And they're freer with their emotional world, more down to earth, less worried about the eyes of society and more inclined to take things way too far.

I can imagine the downstairs servants doing something quite rash if they were pushed too far. Doing something they'd prefer Upstairs not to interfere with. Doing something on impulse. I can imagine them getting upset and staging a coup. Just temporarily of course, then they'd come to their senses I'm sure.

Can you imagine Thomas Barrow in charge? It isn't going to go well.

If the Downton servants were in control of Downton Abbey it could go very badly because they're not used to being in charge and they've had very little experience with power. They're smart people. However their vista is small, they simply don't have the big picture the family upstairs has. It's easy to see they're likely to handle their new power rather clumsily.

GET OUT OF MY WAY

And clumsily is one of the milder words for how the Downstairs Brain handles power when it stages a coup of its own.

When your hippocampus tells your amygdala (both parts of the Limbic system) there's a perceived threat, a flight, fight or freeze situation, then your amygdala sends out a signal that stops the rational brain from interfering while Downstairs gets into protection mode.

Downstairs needs all hands on deck and all available energy in order to give the possible threat its absolute and undivided attention. It doesn't want the distractions of rational, thinking Upstairs Brain interfering when it has such urgent work to do. There is no time for thinking twice, weighing up options or getting into analysis. Nor is there time to be concerned if the response is appropriate. The Downstairs Brain is all go, go, go, action! It wants to get on with its reactive stuff unhindered.

In fact, and this is really alarming, the Downstairs Brain can take control in milliseconds.

Our Downstairs Brain gets information milliseconds before the more rational Upstairs brain, which is why if Downstairs thinks danger is nigh, it has time to shut down Upstairs. It's as though it took out scissors and cut the connection.

FLIPPING YOUR LID

Dan Siegel calls this Downstairs takeover Flipping Your Lid. There are other common names including Amygdala Hijack, a term coined by Daniel Goleman in his 1995 runaway bestseller *'Emotional Intelligence'*. You might know it as losing control or freaking out.

It works something like this. Imagine you're walking down a street at night when suddenly you hear a dog barking, very aggressively and very close. Straight away the limbic system in your brain is on the job, pumping a shot of adrenalin into your bloodstream. Instantly you are alert and focused, the hair on your neck bristling and your heart pumping faster. You look around, eyes wide and pupils dilating, but you can't see the dog in the inky-black shadows around you. At this point the limbic system decides this is a threat and it hijacks your upstairs brain.

There is no time for analysing or weighing options. Before you know it, your legs kick into action and speed you to the other end of the street. Safe and panting, you finally look around. The dog is nowhere to be seen. You decide to take a few deep breaths to calm yourself as you continue your journey.

Now, in this case, you had good reason to run but that is not always the case. If someone cuts you off in traffic and your sudden impulse is to ram their car, it's not what you'd call a reasonable response. But people do crazy stuff like that all the time, right?

Well, not you or me of course.

THE CHAIN REACTION

It's all got to do with what your brain perceives as a threat, and that depends on your past experiences. If you were bullied at school and years later someone cuts you off on the road, then you might feel like you're being bullied once again.

Suddenly all those old impulses to get back at that bully can trigger you to flip you lid. You won't have planned this and you may not have seen it coming but the next thing you know, you're pushing your foot on the accelerator. It's a disaster in the making.

ALMOST DEAD

I want to demonstrate, in case you haven't experienced this yourself, how profoundly the Downstairs Brain can affect you. I experienced the freeze part of the takeover years ago when Phil and I made titanium jewellery for a living.

To set the scene: We ran our jewellery manufacturing business from a very large shed in our backyard. The workroom door faced the back of our house about 20 metres away. As part of the manufacturing process we used a lethal mix of acids.

We knew this mix was ridiculously dangerous. We'd read about a scientist dropping a small container of it on his lap and dying because there was no way to stop the acid causing a chemical reaction that would go on to strip the calcium from his body. It put most people off working with titanium and our mix was an extra special one we'd designed ourselves. We had it made by a local chemical engineer and it was stored safely in our workroom in a 40 litre airtight demijohn inside a sealed plastic box.

For some reason we decided to change the mix and after our new batch of acid was delivered we stored it in the usual way. Two days later Phil noticed vapour escaping from the box. The acid was overheating, something that had never happened before. Phil loosened the lid then took the demijohn outside into the pouring rain where he thought it would cool down.

Even now, just writing about what happened next, I'm feeling sick. The horror of what almost occurred is still with me and I can barely believe our luck that it didn't end in disaster.

Instead of cooling down the new mix just got hotter and hotter but neither of us noticed. Phil went back to the workroom and I was in the house getting dinner. We thought we'd avoided a drama and assumed the acid would cool down now the pressure was released and the rain was falling on it.

Phil was in the workroom and I was setting the large family table on our back verandah when I noticed acid spurting from the container and was aghast to see the container was almost round, it was obviously about to blow. The door that Phil was about to walk out of, to come for dinner, was just a metre from the acid. I didn't know where the kids were. In with Phil? In another part of the shed? Were they somewhere nearby about to

Those were the days when I still cooked.

run into the backyard or come out of another of the shed's doors as they too came in for dinner?

I knew that any minute our acid cocktail would explode, covering anyone who walked out that door and there'd be nothing a doctor could do to save them if it happened.

I froze. I couldn't speak and I couldn't warn him or yell for the kids. I tried to scream but nothing happened. I doubt my mouth even moved. I was locked and frozen. Forty litres of deadly acid was about to shower the vicinity and I could do nothing.

Unbeknownst to me, Phil had decided to check the acid. Wisely, he'd also decided that taking a peek out the door, without opening it fully, would be a good idea. He saw what was happening and shut the door just as the container blew up. Fortunately none of the kids were nearby when it went.

I was so traumatised by the almost-calamity, I couldn't bear Phil to even relate the story to anyone for a couple of years.

GETTING RID OF REASON

When Downstairs takes control, the potential for disaster is huge because, in most situations, getting rid of Upstairs Brain is a major tactical error. When you flip your lid, or freeze as I did, your limbic system just got rid of a whole range of things that are essential to maintaining life, keeping good relationships and staying out of jail such as:

Language

The ability to calm fear

Information processing

Compassion

Self-understanding

Empathy

Considered decision making

Morality

Attuned listening

Emotional control

Your understanding of what's appropriate in the situation

If your Downstairs Brain is in charge, you're all reaction and emotion without the benefit of brakes, wisdom or care. Listening skills have disappeared, you can't truly fathom what someone is saying to you. You've entered the twilight zone where bad things happen. Your whole system is on alert and you're likely to jump at shadows and see almost anything anyone says or does as a threat.

Remember 'Lost In Space'? It's like your brain is the robot saying 'Danger, Will Robinson, Danger!'

Now here's the really important bit: When you're Downstairs it may take only a minute to ruin a relationship forever.

Don't get me wrong, Downstairs isn't all bad. Remember Downstairs keeps you alive, makes sex fabulous and a host of other great things. It just isn't all that smart to let Downstairs take charge and call the shots – especially while driving or relating to anyone.

Yet for some people it's normal to attempt to solve problems while Downstairs, that's how they do most conflict.

DOWNSTAIRS DUELLERS

I think of these these people as Downstairs Duellers. They often have volcanic relationships and a simple disagreement can easily turn into a major drama.

We once had neighbours like this. Gorgeous people who tried to solve their problems by shouting, crying, screaming, name-calling and freaking out.

When they moved in nearby, it was very early days in their relationship. Their first big fight was astonishingly loud and I'm guessing it was quite a shock for them to find themselves in a domestic of that nature. She knocked on our door the next day, mortified and apologising profusely for the noise. Some weeks later there was another fight. This time she didn't speak of it. Initially we'd hear their emotional fracas every few weeks, then it became much more regular, an almost predictable pattern.

For years she never spoke of their fights again. It was the elephant in the room when we saw them. An elephant that was breaking their hearts and stomping out their love.

Some relationships, be they couples, friendships, families or colleagues, return again and again to situations that push them into corners and invite a visit from the Downstairs team.

Downstairs duelling doesn't solve problems, it just throws them around for a while.

When Downstairs does take over, your guard comes down, emotions get aired, and words get said. Words you've never uttered before, things you thought privately suddenly get said publicly. In time, you calm down.

If you didn't do anything too crazy while Downstairs, then maybe you feel a sense of relief you got it off your chest. Maybe you feel the air has cleared and the tension is gone. And, for a while, things may seem better.

> You might feel relief now you have that 'something' off your chest. However, the person who had to hear those words might still be reeling from them weeks later.

The problem with this pattern is that, at the time of the conflict, everyone involved is way too emotional and actual issues don't get addressed in a way that moves things forward.

In time the unsolved problems can escalate and the duelling can worsen. Contrary to popular opinion, letting it all hang out and airing your resentments doesn't help your relationships. Instead research by Dr Gottman shows it increases anger and makes further explosions likely.

TAMING THE MONSTER

In my ideal world, I'd live my life with my Upstairs Brain in control at all times. My reason, calm and compassion would stay firmly in place and when it came to managing conflict, misunderstandings, betrayals and the like, I'd always be wise, patient and terribly mature.

Instead, I'm part of the real world, flawed, totally inconsistent and still vulnerable to giving someone the finger as well as the usual slip-ups, shoutings and shit choices.

If only I was living in my ideal world

The wonderful thing about your brain, the thing that has been wildly helpful for me to know, is it sticks to well-worn paths. Those neural pathways are created by what you think.

When you repeatedly think, behave and react a certain way, eventually your brain just goes 'Oh, fabulous, this is what you want me to do. Let's switch on autopilot and let this baby run'.

And, seemingly without you having to think or make effort, your brain will default to that behaviour/thinking/reaction at the next appropriate opportunity. Your brain loves a good default because it saves your brain energy.

From what I understand, the outcomes of defaulting to often-used pathways are twofold. Firstly, the more a neural pathway is used the more dominant it becomes. The more dominant a pathway the more your brain defaults to it. It's all too easy to accidentally end up with a super-highway that your brain continually defaults to. You can see there's potential for problems depending on how you've been thinking.

I realised the more time I spent being pissed off, angry, reactive, complaining, negative, stressed, sad, hopeless, anxious, fearful and the like, the more my brain would default to those thoughts.

And the more likely I'd be to behave in ways consistent with those thoughts.

MORE SWITCHED ON

Secondly, areas of the brain that are often used can become larger, more 'switched-on' and more available for use.

My brain said 'No way!' when I asked it about learning French

For example, if you decided to learn French, yet had no experience of speaking French, it's likely your brain will have very few pathways for French. It must create some new pathways and that takes some work. Work your brain would prefer not to do. It already has enough to deal with without you coming along and deciding French is a great idea.

Depending on your age, your affinity for language, how frequent the lessons are, how much you practise and a host of other things, you'd have, in time, pathways for French and it would become easier for you. If you'd learned just enough French to get you through a short trip to France your brain may not retain the new language for long.

However, if you decided to speak French all the time that area of your brain would become quite developed and very easy for you to access. Speaking French might even become effortless.

JUGGLERS, TAXI DRIVERS & MUSICIANS

Researchers at Harvard, Yale and the Massachusetts Institute of Technology found people who meditated increased thickness in parts of their brains that deal with attention and processing sensory input. Changes in brain size can be seen with London taxi drivers. Their memory area enlarges because they've had to store all the streets of London in it. Other research shows jugglers increase the size of their visual and motor areas while, not surprisingly, musicians increase the size of the music area of their brains.

The last thing I wanted was a hyper-developed, over-active, ready to leap-in-a-single-bound, super-ripped Downstairs Brain. I already had one of those and it wasn't serving me well. I needed to get more muscle power to my Upstairs Brain. I was pretty sure if I had a brain that defaulted to 'reasoned calm' during stress, my life could be a bit easier to handle.

I wanted ways to ensure I'd spend less time Downstairs wreaking havoc in my relationships with others, and my relationship with myself, so I found some useful ways to help myself and I'll cover them in the next chapter.

THE PRACTICE

Read A Book About Your Brain

Getting acquainted with your brain is amazing. Check out the back of this book for a link to my recommended reads.

My friend Mary-Lou suggested you watch Downton Abbey instead, and I agree it might be the more fun option. Take your pick.

'What do
sad people have in
common?
It seems they have all built a
shrine to the past and often go
there and do a strange
wail and worship.
What is the beginning of
Happiness?
It is to stop being so
religious
like that.'

HAFEZ

9

THE QUEST TO STAY UPSTAIRS

I've run at issues all my life. I must have thought, 'Here is an issue. Get rid of it', and gone in full blast. I can see now that perhaps I, and the people I wanted to sort out issues with, might have been better served if I'd focused on how to handle the issue calmly rather than focusing only on the issue.

Being calm, mature and communicative in the face of big issues hasn't really been my strong suit in the past. You can take heart if this has been your history too, because I've found some simple ways to be less reactive and I'll share all in this chapter.

STOPPING THE DOWNSTAIRS TAKEOVER

As I said, no one liked she-monster, least of all me, and I wanted to find a way, or many ways if needed, to stop the Downstairs takeover when it began to happen.

You'd think this would be difficult, long and complicated yet, in reality, this one was easier to deal with than I had imagined.

I went to a course, paid a lot of money and learned to tell myself to STOP.

Okay, I know, it sounds like I got scammed. Surely the solution couldn't be that simple? Well, yes and no. It was during this course I first became acquainted with my brain, so right away I knew it was money well spent.

It was this backdrop of brain science that opened my eyes to what was happening and this understanding made saying stop the first sensible step.

On the course, I was taught to stop whatever train of thought was distressing me and quickly change to a different train of thought, one that was more rewarding. It worked surprisingly well once I got the hang of it.

Once I'd experienced the shift and started to really 'get' the idea that I did have a choice, I didn't need the more formal 'stop and switch' process, it started to come a little more naturally. Mind you, I still have to make the choice even today.

After four to five weeks of practising the switch, I could usually shift almost instantly and this was partly because I was less attached to thinking what I was feeling was the truth. It's so easy to be under the misapprehension that our feelings are the truth and that we cannot change them.

I do remember telling my kids to choose their emotional state when they were younger so I must have recognised this truth at one time. However, like many things, along the way I seem to have forgotten it or maybe I found it impossible to do. Either way I've had to learn this all over again.

I think because these neural defaults happen with lightning speed, they're almost instant, its easy to be unaware of having made any choice.

The 'stop and select emotion' practice lets me see the process and interrupt it.

While the issue that had prompted me to attend the course in the first place was depression rather than my struggles with Downstairs eruptions, I found once I'd learned to change pathways more easily I could use this trick pretty effectively to reduce my chances of flipping my lid.

I also started to see my excuses for what they were. I couldn't really continue to blame others for how I was feeling and this resulted in a shift in the scripts and stories I ran in my head. I'm now far less likely to say things like:

'I can't help it, that's just how I feel,' or 'She makes me so angry'.

I have come to see I'm blaming and excusing when I try to put the cause of my emotional state on to someone else.

One thing I have noticed, though, is I have to spend time building the calmer, more positive, easy-going pathways, if I want them to be available to me when I need them.

The brain isn't going to divert to pathways that aren't there.

The Stop bit is the easy bit. It takes a while to learn to choose a different emotion.

Later in this chapter I'll suggest some tools that might help you develop more control of your Downstairs Brain. There are also useful resources on my website, and a good psychologist will have many skills to teach you.

GETTING BACK UPSTAIRS QUICKLY

Not that I always say Stop of course. Sometimes I don't, and I find myself on the edge of, or in, the freak-out zone.

Once there, it's very useful if you can get out fast. Dan Siegel's book has a great suggestion that he calls *Name it to Tame It.* While the book is referring to using this technique with kids it works with adults too. (Seriously, if you have kids, read *'The Whole Brain Child'* you'll love me for recommending it.)

Name It To Tame It. Dr Dan suggests (when dealing with a child) first you hug them to help calm them, then you ask them what they're feeling. As they search for the answer they're automatically going back to Upstairs Brain because they're analysing and will have to use language to give you the answer.

A version of *'Name It To Tame It'* I use for myself includes saying soothing words to myself such as 'It's okay, you can handle this.'

Then I identify the feeling, and sometimes it's hard to admit, even to myself, what I'm feeling. Angry might be easy to own up to however jealous or vengeful are much harder for me to face.

As is 'bruised ego'.

Once the feeling is identified I'm usually in a place where I can switch to a different feeling. If, for some reason, that isn't successful then I start to analyse something else in order to distract my brain from its emotional place. Provided the distraction isn't anything to do with why I'm in my Downstairs Brain, this usually works. If I'm with others, it's best if I don't resume the conversation until I'm completely calm.

GO TO BED ANGRY

To get completely calm, I may need a total break from the conversation. I'm not a fan of the old adage, 'Never go to bed angry'. I'd much rather go to bed angry than risk saying something I'll regret while trying to sort out a conflict when I'm tired or feeling 'downstairsy'.

I'm not saying I switch seamlessly from, say, panic to feeling bloody marvelous. Sometimes that happens, though more often it doesn't. I've just moved myself out of that very reactive place. To get to 'bloody marvelous', I'd have to do a bit more work

STAYING UPSTAIRS

This is the area where I've concentrated my efforts. I'm not sure if some people are 'naturally anxious' and some more 'naturally calm'. There'll be many theories I'm sure. If there are naturally anxious people, I think it's likely I'm one of them, though my mother would disagree. She doesn't remember me being anxious as a child.

My dad was a 'business adventurer'. He'd jump from real estate to being a travel agent and then buy a farm and farm it. He seemed to lose interest in each new venture when he'd made it very successful. This meant I had to change schools regularly and maybe it was this continual entrance in to new environments, always being the odd one out and the desperate quest to find new friends that left me a worrywart.

Or maybe it was absolutely nothing to do with those moves, my childhood or my parents. Who knows, and in the end, who cares. It doesn't matter how I developed a very engaged and reactive Downstairs Brain. It matters that I find some ways to calm it down in general, so it's less likely to stage a takeover.

To do that I had to build some more positive pathways to which my brain could default. I had to make some of those super-highway neural pathways that rushed maybe to panic, maybe to anger, maybe to rejection, a little less dominant. They were not serving me well.

Like anything, rewiring your own brain isn't a quick-fix. It takes time. However, I did find I noticed improvements fairly quickly. It took quite a while though before there was any natural default. And, even now, I have to be attentive to where my thoughts are wandering.

YOUR FANTASTIC PLASTIC BRAIN

Your plastic brain is rewiring and responding all the time to information, to what you say, think and do, and is also being influenced by music, games, media and even what you talk about when you're with friends.

Anything you decide to take up to rewire your brain has to be practised and become part of your day-to-day life.

I find it very hard to create and stick to any sort of new diet, exercise program, writing schedule or even personal journaling. In fact personal schedules or routines of any kind feel a little claustrophobic to me. I join gyms, classes, groups and have yet to manage to stick to any of them for any serious length of time, let alone incorporate them into my life.

Weirdly enough, and in total contrast to this, there is little I love more than planning and scheduling.

Give me a large event, let me plan it, design it, create it down to the tiniest detail and I'm in heaven. That thing will run like clockwork, yet feel natural and fun.

I was Creative Director for the very first *'Wired for Wonder'* event in 2013. I was talking to one of the more internationally renowned speakers and I must have said something to her about how tight the schedule was because I remember her saying to me, 'Oh, you'll be running an hour late by end of day one. That's what happens at events'.

My response was to challenge her to a bet. 'I bet you $100 that we don't run even a minute late at any point over the whole two days.' I won the bet as I knew I would.

Clockwork at work, and almost never late to anything, that's me, so you'd think I'd be able to have some sort of timetable at home. Not so much. Phil and I even find it hard to schedule any sort of regular formal work meeting and it's just the two of us!

All this is to let you know that I'm not one of those people who easily adopt a new discipline or practice. Yet I was quickly able to make strides in rewiring my brain and to create a calmer and happier life for myself . This may give you hope, because if someone who can't get to the gym on a regular basis can pull it off, it's more than likely you can too.

Read happier on the days I practice what I preach!

THE SIMPLEST GAME CHANGER

For the past seven years I've been on this quest to find the gold for change and quite frankly, I found it. There is nothing I can find, have tried, have read about or researched that quite matches the rewiring power of gratitude.

I found gratitude practice so effective it was hard to believe what I was experiencing could be true. So, in true Toni style, I started researching it, reading everything I could.

In 2012, Phil and I travelled the globe interviewing leaders in the fields of neuroscience, psychology and spirituality as well as researchers in happiness and gratitude. We had the privilege of talking to, interviewing and often spending time with some incredible people including Gretchen Rubin, Mattieu Ricard and Olivia Newton-John. We even scored footage with Dr John Medina.

Gratitude is a fascinating subject that I'll touch on very briefly now and revisit later in the book. As a tool to help you stay calm it is magic because it rewires your brain and helps you experience the world as a less confronting place.

If you want Downstairs to serve you well, then start with gratitude and appreciation practices. Write in a journal, say grace or take photos, they're popular ways to approach gratitude. My favourite, and the one I believe to be the most effective, is to write notes, letters, texts and emails that express your appreciation of others.

I'm pretty sure I've never upset anyone by telling them how great they are.

AND THE SCIENCE SAYS

Of course I'm always looking into what research is showing about how to do life well, how to keep calm and enjoy this brief time on earth.

As far as gaining control of your Downstairs Brain, there are many things, apart from practising gratitude, you can do, and a few stand out as being very effective.

Meditation: Ooh, you knew I was going to put it in here somewhere didn't you? Well yes, of course, there's a reason that absolutely everyone seems to be talking about it. The benefits are ridiculous and by meditating you are actually learning to control your limbic system. So it's great. Do it if you can. It will definitely be a help to your relationships, well unless you piss off your family by meditating instead of doing the dishes.

I've seen this sort of stuff, it happens!

I am, so far, a total new-age failure in that I just haven't been able to sit still long enough to meditate. I've tried, really, I've given it many tries. I'm very aware meditation is transformative and important and I'm sure I'll get there one day. For the moment though, I avoid the stares, lectures and gasps of shock from the wellness peeps I hang around with, by refusing to admit to anyone that I don't meditate. So please, if you don't mind, would you keep my admission to yourself.

Get in The Zone: Spending time in the zone, the activity that takes you out of yourself and into a place of flow is another crucial thing you can do to improve both your relationships and your limbic control. Being in the zone, be it surfing, drawing, dancing, playing music or gardening, has been shown to be very calming for your nervous system. These days, they're even treating PTSD with surfing classes. If you want healing, a peaceful heart, a well mind and body, then taking time out for play. Taking time to be in the zone is anything but selfish.

Exercise: Exercise is a very quick way to calm down, use up those bits of energy that are threatening to burst out, and also improve your fitness.

Your brain will be affected by your level of fitness and lying around the house has never been shown to improve mood or brain function.

Eat Well: Again, this isn't rocket science. You want great chemicals swimming around your system and especially in your brain. Junk food is full of not-so-great chemicals so that might not be your best choice of food on a regular basis. The research is pretty clear, lots of alcohol and caffeine aren't great for keeping calm. Don't freak out though, I'm not espousing some rigid adherence to a special super-health diet as that would be hilarious coming from a woman whose enjoyment of a meal can be ruined by the appearance of a vegetable.

Dear vegetarians, I love you. I'd love to love vegetables too, however I think they just don't love me.

Our bodies are unique, what works for some won't work for another. You'll find loads of conflicting articles and research, so you'll have to work out what foods affect your mood by experimenting. More and more doctors and naturopaths are specialising in the food/mood connection, so you'll be able to get help if you want some.

Getting plenty of zinc and B6 has worked a treat for me.

Eat to feel great, enjoy the foods that make you feel good in the long term.

Watch Funny Films: Laughter is so great for your brain. Do something to make yourself laugh as often as you can.

Hang Out With Happy People: This could be more important than you think. The people you hang out with will influence your behaviour, often quite subconsciously. Make sure you spend lots of time with people who bring peace and joy into your life, and minimal time with those who bring you down or stress you out.

Read Dr Dan's Books: Dr Dan Siegel has a range of fabulous books on this subject including many to do with kids and teenagers. I've listed many of them in the booklist on my website: www.tonipowell.me/what-a-feeling-book-list

It makes sense to me the more you improve your mental health the more likely it is your relationships will fare well.

THE PRACTICE

Stop and Look Around

As Ferris Bueller said, 'Life moves pretty fast. If you don't stop and look around once in awhile, you could miss it'.

'To keep in love
is also a business of
some importance, to which
both man and wife must bring
kindness and goodwill - a
beautiful contest
of wisdom and
generosity.'

ROBERT LOUIS STEVENSON

PARAPHRASED FROM

VIRGINIBUS PUERISQUE AND OTHER PAPERS

10

THE BANK

Two years after we got married we were living, temporarily, in a town that was in the grip of a severe drought.

When we turned on the taps nothing much came out, if we were lucky we might get a brown dribble. It was a rural town and the local wildlife was desperate for water too, so they came into town to see what we had. There were snakes everywhere and for a while, stacks of huge grasshoppers. There'd been a tiger snake in the courtyard that Phil had narrowly missed stepping on while carrying our daughter. Tiger snakes are nasty. While large huntsman spiders in your house or car aren't all that unusual for Australia, having a car with lots and lots of large huntsmen spiders living in it, was.

It was a bit like being in an old testament plague.

One day Phil and I had some sort of fight. I don't recall what prompted that particular drama. Was it because I didn't love him? I didn't, but that was nothing new. Was being a mum overwhelming me? Of course it was, all the time. Was it other issues? I don't know. For the most part, we'd been fairly happy together. He was kind and easy to get on with, plus we'd been quizzing people and working on our relationship for all that time.

Whatever the reason I decided it was all too hard and walked out. I said he could have the baby and I'd take the car. I intended to leave permanently.

Until I drove off in the car that is.

I'd only driven a couple of blocks when I remembered the spiders. Shit! Spiders, there were spiders in the car, spiders that would crawl on me while I was driving. Spiders that would cause an accident when they fell into my lap while speeding down the motorway at 100k. Spiders that would cause me to have a spectacular car crash! Unhappy though I was, death by spider didn't have any appeal, so I had to drive back to Phil and try to work it out, at least for the next few months.

Did I mention my gift for imagining disaster?

AND LOVE BEGAN

Somehow we ended up at a counsellor, a guy in his 40s. I can't imagine I wanted to go and I find it hard to believe Phil organised it, so it's a mystery to me how we came to be sitting across from this man. I was angry and really only had one point to make, 'Well I don't love him. There's not much use us talking to you.'

The counsellor ignored me and focused on Phil. 'Do you love her?' he asked.

'Yes,' Phil said.

'Would you still love her if she didn't ever love you? Would you still want to be with her?'

Again, Phil answered in the affirmative.

Did the world stop? Was I bowled over? Did I say anything? I have no idea. I only know that day was the day love started for me. His answer turned a key and the love began.

For the next nine or ten years, we skipped along merrily, exploring the world and exploring each other. Maybe somewhat too often, as we added another three children in there somewhere. We kept up our 'research' and our quizzing of couples and our reading of books until we came across a book in 1989 called '*His Needs, Her Needs, Building an Affair Proof Marriage*' by Willard F. Harley Jr. That book changed so much for us.

Just a little caveat here. The edition I read was a rather conservative book, first published in 1986, with some concepts I had to leap over in order to get to the exceptional stuff. When we found this book so helpful to us, we recommended it to lots of people and had very mixed feedback. Even back then I found some of this book rather old-fashioned, though I imagine his work has moved with the times and is much updated now.

The author, Willard F. Harley Jr., has a long history as a psychologist, once running a string of mental health practices in Minnesota so large he had 100 staff. He's reputedly saved thousands of marriages and currently has a website called Marriage Builders. I had a quick look through it and there are lots of free resources for you to sift through (some look wonderful). Take what works and leave what doesn't sit well with you.

SIMPLE BRILLIANCE

What Harley taught us is so simple I cannot even believe I had to learn it. However, I did, and maybe you can benefit from it too. Here's the basics of it:

> Each of us has a 'love bank' where we keep track of how people make us feel. If you make someone feel valued you've made a deposit. Lots of deposits make love grow.

Easy! However, if you make someone feel devalued or less, then you've made a withdrawal. Lots of withdrawals and love diminishes.

Too many withdrawals and you get into overdraft and love turns to hate.

One of the big issues is that simply living together makes constant, sometimes even massive, withdrawals you might not even be aware of.

Clothes left on the floor? *Withdrawal.*

Left the toilet seat up? *Withdrawal.*

Didn't take the trash out? *Withdrawal.*

Bad breath? *Might be a withdrawal.*

Forgets your birthday? *Withdrawal.*

Hogs the remote? *Withdrawal.*

Nags you? *Withdrawal.*

This stuff happens with friends, family and everyone in your life.

Forget to return the books I loaned you? *Withdrawal.*

Rarely say thanks? *Big withdrawal*

Arrive late to our meetings? *Withdrawal.*

Never call? *Withdrawal.*

Talk about yourself too much? *Withdrawal.*

Don't invite us back when we had you over? *Withdrawal.*

Always manage to get out of paying for coffee? *Withdrawal.*

The things that make deposits are the things that make people feel valued and herein lies the problem, and happily, the solution. For the most part you follow the old adage, 'Do unto others as you would have them do unto you'. Which sounds wonderful and is actually pretty great. However, the problem is what makes you feel valued is not necessarily what makes someone else feel valued.

You have to remember you're seeing, hearing, and understanding the world quite differently to your other. You are, to a degree, foreigners. Your language may not be understood by all the other foreigners with whom you have relationships. You might be making cultural faux pas without even realising.

For 12 years that is exactly what Phil and I were doing.

I love breakfast in bed. I love, love, love it. Yet for 12 years, Phil would rarely give it to me because it was inconceivable to him that anyone could possibly enjoy eating in bed. It seemed dirty, who would want crumbs in their bed? Why eat off your lap when someone had gone to the trouble of designing a table and chairs expressly for comfortable eating? He didn't get it at all.

Just last night he found pork crackling in the bed. He held it up and looked quite accusing.

Whenever I wanted to make clear to Phil he was the light of my life I'd make him breakfast in bed. I'd be confused by his lack of excitement about my carefully decorated tray.

On our first Christmas together, he bought me a spinning wheel. He was baffled by my lack of interest. But guess who liked to spin? Hint, it wasn't me. Years later he couldn't understand my less than delighted reaction when he gave me long nose pliers for Christmas. He maintained they were perfect for me, and they truly were. They were expensive Swedish ones and he thought, as we manufactured jewellery for a living, they would make my job easier and they did. However, they were a business expense and it felt a bit like getting a vacuum cleaner for Christmas.

Tich Naht Hahn has some stunning quotes. I thought this one was perfect for here:

> *'To love without knowing how to love wounds the person we love.'*

Harley's book made us aware just because it says 'love' to you doesn't mean it says 'love' to someone else. If you want to make deposits with someone you have to discover what makes them feel valued.

We've made this into a cool game at our workshops and people can be surprised to find their version of giving love isn't necessarily appreciated by everyone in the room. They usually think their version will be the exception. How could anyone not like something that we would love?

DO UNTO OTHERS AS THEY'D LIKE DONE UNTO THEM

Long friendships, good marriages, strong family relationships and even good work relationships happen when you make an effort to learn everything you can about the other person.

Those that are Magicians at relationships learn what the other person wants and gives it to them without them having to ask for it. They're aware that being forced to ask is an automatic withdrawal.

Then there are those who are Muggles at relationships. They cruise along thinking that if it's love, it's love and all shall work well because it's love. Muggles can be laid back when it comes to investing in relationships. They have a bit of 'they love me so it will be ok' attitude which is fine while the love bank is in the black. Get that little piggy in the red though and suddenly all hell breaks loose.

The *'His Needs, Her Needs'* book came with an *Emotional Needs Questionnaire* in the back of the book. The instructions were to photocopy the questionnaire twice, so you each had one, and then go off to separate rooms to fill them in. Then you came back together and swapped, so you could better understand each other's needs.

Phil's answers caused me to ask a question I'd never thought to ask him before. I'd never asked because I assumed I knew the answer. The question was, 'Why did you marry me?'

The answer I thought I knew he'd give was 'Because we were having a baby'. I had always believed he'd married me because he was that sort of guy. A good guy. In my mind he did what he thought was the right thing to do and he did it with grace. I didn't think he regretted his decision and I knew he loved me, however it hadn't crossed my mind there was another answer.

The real answer to that question was, 'Because I wanted to. You are the one person I wanted to marry. I chose you.'

This answer was unexpected, delightful and healing. He hadn't married me because he'd had to. He hadn't married me to do the right thing. He'd married me because he wanted to, because he adored me.

This changed things on a deep level for me. I was finally home.

The *Emotional Needs Questionnaire* also helped us understand each other and understand how to make room for, and meet, each other's needs in ways we hadn't been doing until then. To find out more about the questionnaire just check out the page at the end of my book that mentions buckets.

MAKING MOMENTUM

In a situation like a long marriage you can 'learn each other' very well. However, it is the Love Bank that keeps the momentum humming. It's all very well to know what Phil needs and know how to meet those needs. It's not much use knowing it if I don't bother doing anything about it. I think the Love Bank idea helped me see what I have with Phil and indeed, what I have with any of my friends and family, is very fragile and can easily be lost through neglect.

Love takes attention. It is built and maintained by conscious care, by getting in the ring and playing the contest of generosity as often as you can.

Willard F. Harley Jr. taught us something simple that enabled us to take our 'okay happyish' relationship and turn it into a very happy one. This continues to work provided we practise love and generosity through making those deposits.

MAKING DEPOSITS

Many of the things that make deposits are so ordinary they can seem insignificant and you forget you have them at your disposal. I'll run through a few of these, so you've got something to start with straight away.

HUGS

Hugs, especially longer ones, don't just say 'I care'. There are studies showing all sorts of benefits. I'll mention just a few of the many ways hugs can contribute to better relationships:

Oxytocin Release: Even a six second hug releases oxytocin. This is the bonding hormone mothers get flooded with when they give birth and the same hormone lovers are swimming in during those first few delicious months together. Apart from being a 'feel good' hormone, oxytocin will increase empathy, lower social anxiety, increase trust and make you more likely to take selfless action for others. Also, oxytocin helps heal feelings of loneliness, isolation and anger. If you're in any sort of relationship you've gotta love that.

Increase Immunity and Decrease Stress: Research out of Carnegie Mellon University in 2014 found hugs can help you fight off infection, and are effective for reducing stress.

Hugs Calm Your Nervous System: Depending on who you hug of course, hugs can make you feel safer and also have an effect similar to laughter on your nervous system, you feel calmer afterward. Apparently hugs can relax muscles and decrease perception of pain. Hugs also reduce your fear response.

LONGER HUGS

There are many more benefits to hugs and yet we often only bother with a fleeting one that generally doesn't do any of the above. Twenty second hugs, which are quite long compared to how long you might usually hug, are supposed to be an ideal length.

After reading some of the research about hugging, I decided to give it a try to see whether it could help with an awkward situation. Someone I cared about had become distant. Stuff had happened and she wasn't someone who liked to discuss emotional things, so talking about it wasn't an option. So I started giving her longer hugs, just a bit longer at first and gradually, for a period of months, I hugged longer and longer.

Then I started holding her gaze for longer as well. Whatever the problem was has disappeared and years later we still have a very close relationship even though I'm no longer the hug-stalker. I just went back to a more normal amount of hugging after everything was well again.

Apparently humans have need of multiple hugs a day for optimum health, depending on the article you read, that number is anything from four to eight to twenty.

SMILING

Again smiling appears so ordinary it hardly seems like it should rate a mention as a way of making deposits. Yet smiling is incredibly powerful and it's something you might be forgetting to do in an intentional way.

Imagine this for a minute. You've been called to your boss's office and when you enter the door his face lights up and he gives you the biggest smile you've seen for a while.

How would you feel if your boss smiled at you like that? What would you think? What has been communicated?

If I had a boss who smiled at me like that I'd feel like I was approved of, accepted, well regarded and appreciated. I'd feel great even though he has said nothing.

Or imagine this, a child is tugging at his mother's jumper, asking her to come and look at something. She's on the computer, she's busy and very focused. Instead of continuing to look at the computer and saying, 'I'll be there in a minute', she stops what she's doing, turns and looks at the child fully and then gives him her biggest, longest smile before she tells him she'll be there in a minute.

To do the opposite of either of these takes the same amount of effort and makes instant withdrawals. What would this child feel when his mummy smiled at him like that? I'd be willing to bet the child would feel valued, loved and cared for.

Which isn't what he'd feel if she hadn't turned and smiled, yet she has said nothing different to him. That child will run off feeling secure and trusting his mum is going to come and see what he wants to show her. He'll know he's important to her.

In both these scenarios, the people smiling have made huge deposits because they've made the people they've smiled at feel great. It cost them nothing, took virtually no planning and was quick to do.

On top of that, smiling has some ridiculously great side-effects, some are similar to those of hugging and then there are a whole lot just specific to smiling.

Smiling people are viewed as:

More intelligent

More attractive

More trustworthy

Younger looking

When you're stressed, and you probably are most days if you live a normal modern life, then you might be forgetting to smile at the people you live with, your child's teacher, the person who gets coffee etc. It's a quick free way to make deposits and has the added benefit of being contagious. You'll cheer everyone up.

In fact you can smile intentionally, just you, alone in a room and immediately decrease your stress levels and release feel good hormones.

Which brings me to a very relevant point. One of the reasons smiling is so contagious is because our brains are wired to 'mirror' emotions so we can feel what others are feeling. For example, when we cry in movies, our brains are reading and experiencing the emotions of the actors. Then the brain gives you the feelings that go with that expression, so you then understand what's going on.

The opposite of smiling is true too. You know how it feels when someone enters a room when they're in a bad mood. They bring dark clouds that make everyone in the room on edge. Your emotional life continually seeps into the emotional lives of those around you. Is your emotional life making deposits or withdrawals?

GAZING

A third ridiculously simple thing to do and one that also has crazy power, is gazing into the eyes of someone you love. This is great to do with a child, your partner or someone you are very close to, though can be overwhelming or threatening if you do it with people who aren't very familiar with you. I love what author Martha Beck says:

> *'Basic human contact, the meeting of eyes, the exchanging of words, is to the psyche what oxygen is to the brain. If you're feeling abandoned by the world, interact with anyone you can.'*

TECHNOLOGY

Okay, so there's a lot of stuff about the impact of technology on relationships and some of it is worrying. People are tending toward more narcissism. I read just the other day girls in the

UK are spending five hours a week taking selfies. If that isn't narcissistic I don't know what is.

I worry that unless children get enough face time with real faces, they may not develop the skills they need to read emotional information. We learn a lot of things by looking at faces.

Certainly it's easy to feel rejected by others when they prefer their computer or phone. It's bloody annoying and can be incredibly disrespectful when people pull out phones in social situations. If you want to make someone feel like they don't matter to you just start texting someone else when you're with them.

However technology is also a brilliant way to help your loved ones feel valued.

CALL FOR NO REASON

Refrain from talking about your stuff for the whole call. Just tell them you were thinking of them. It's quick, easy and meaningful. Or call them to ask about whatever it is you know is hard for them. Or call to let them brag about something. 'Hey, weren't you starting your new job this week? Tell me the story of how you got it again. It's such a great story.'

Likewise, it's easy to text or email just to check in, just to say 'You're amazing', or just to let them know they matter. You could even try texting someone about one of their good points maybe along the lines of, 'Maree was talking about how caring her mum is today and I was reminded of how caring you are. You are exceptionally caring. I'm the luckiest. I love you, mum.'

This sort of text will make any mum's day.

PRACTICE

The Smile Competition

Get into competition mode and set yourself some goals. Can you cause five people a day to smile? Can you improve on your score and get to 10? The irresistibility of smiles means that it's pretty easy to get someone to smile. You just smile at them.

This competition with yourself, or even with friends, will make you happier, more cheerful and easier to get on with, as well as making you more conscious of your expression. As an added bonus you'll also be limbering up some of the muscle needed for the 'competition of generosity'.

‘Out
beyond ideas
of wrongdoing and
rightdoing
there is a field.
I’ll meet you there.’

RUMI

11

MAGICIANS AND MUGGLES

Magicians do relationships well and Muggles don't. Simple. We'll get to them in a minute, for a moment though, I want to chat about marriage.

'Mawwiage is wot bwings us togevver'

While researching relationships I've discovered there's lots of readily available research and good advice regarding marriage and couples. I've also found, happily, that marriage/couple stuff is almost always relevant to any relationship you have.

Living together as a couple is the pressure cooker test. Think of it like this: if the relationship principle works well under a lot of heat in a closed environment, it will, in all likelihood, work effectively elsewhere.

To be true to the research, marriage and couple relationships will be mentioned all through this chapter. However, it doesn't matter if you're married or not, gay, trans, consciously uncoupled or waiting for some equality in the law, what you get out of this chapter you can take into any relationship. Even the relationship you have with your next-door neighbour and maybe even the one you have with yourself.

These core principles apply to all relationships.

JIGGLEOMETERS, GOTTMAN & GADGETS

About 40 years ago, at the University of Wisconsin, a young mathematics professor and his best friend, Bob Levenson, realised they didn't know how to get along with women. These days, if a guy finds himself in a similar situation, he can just ask his best mate, Mr Google. Fortunately these two didn't have the internet available, so they had to get creative and their creativity has had a positive effect on countless relationships.

What they did was wonderful. Without any theory or hypothesis, an unusual and brilliant place to start research, they began watching married couples to see what it was that made the happy couples into happy couples.

Their work evolved into a groundbreaking study of married couples that eventually established the young maths professor, Dr John Gottman, as the world's leading authority on marriage. He's able to predict if a couple will divorce with more than 90% accuracy, more about this later.

In the 'Love Lab', their campus-based research centre, this daring pair of single men studied couples. They came up with new gadgets, gizmos and coding systems to conduct their studies including a Jiggleometer to measure how much the couples squirmed in their seats.

Can you imagine the fun these guys had inventing these gadgets?

Their studies consisted of videoing the couples as they discussed areas of conflict in their relationships. Later, after showing the couples the videos, they questioned them about their responses. Gottman and Levenson were careful to note and record facial expressions, heart rate and how much the couples sweated during the discussion. They measured the couples' blood velocities and cortisol levels and also took mouth swabs and urine samples to gain further information. More than 3,000 couples were studied.

The researchers found that happy couples do things very differently to unhappy ones.

They were able to identify the things happy couples did and discover what it was that happy couples knew instinctively about relating.

MAGICIANS AND MUGGLES

Somewhere along the way Gottman became the one who made a name for himself in this field. His research yields some disturbing, though not altogether surprising, statistics. Being a math boy at heart, Gottman delivers well on the stats.

Gottman's definition of a happy marriage:

> One that stays together
>
> Where they like and enjoy one another
>
> Where they express high relational satisfaction

According to Dr Gottman, only 18% of couples have the skills to create a happy marriage.

Yes, only 18%!

No wonder the happy-ever-after quest generally leads to such disappointment. Most of us have no idea how to conduct the business of marriage.

Gottman calls this small group, this elite 18% of married people, the Masters.

A total of 50% of marriages observed by Gottman ended in divorce, and a further 16% remained married even though they were unhappy. That's 66%, which is a dismaying number of people whose hopes for a great relationship are dashed on the rocks of 'actually-living-together-long-term'.

Gottman calls this group, the disappointed 66%, the Disasters.

And speaking of names, excuse me for a sec, I have a letter to write:

Dear Dr Gottman,

I love your work, I really do. I tell everyone about it and recommend your books at all my workshops. You're a genius and you've done wonderful things for relationships. Wonderful things. Thank you from the bottom of my heart.

However, I just have one little bone to pick with you and it's Disasters. The name Disasters. This worries me as all those dear people who fall into that group have already had enough go wrong without being further disheartened to find they are Disasters.

For a while I went along with it and put my niggles aside, but really, I can't anymore. I simply can't call them Disasters, yet I want to tell everyone your wisdom on these two groups.

For my work I use Magicians and Muggles, so that no one feels too bad and I get the added bonus of having magic in there.

So I hope you don't mind that, when I'm referring to your two groups, The Masters and The Disasters, I'm going to substitute with the names I use: Magicians and Muggles.

Other than this minor detail, I wouldn't change a thing about your work. As I said, it's wonderful. I'll make sure to tell all my readers to buy your books.

Thanks for listening, Toni

So, dear reader, please note: when I refer to Magicians and Muggles, just for this chapter, I'm referring to Gottman's

Masters and Disasters. When Magicians and Muggles are mentioned elsewhere in this book, it's not in reference to Gottman's research. What Gottman's work clearly shows is:

It's the Magicians who practise the craft of love.

They know the magic words, and the things that will enchant their partner. The Muggles either didn't realise there was a craft involved or maybe just ignored the instructions. No matter, the beautiful thing about all this is that anyone can learn love, and to help the Muggles I put an extra special Love Potion chapter at the end of this book.

NEVER ENDING CONFLICT

It was of great interest to Gottman to note and understand the skills happy couples employed when handling conflict.

Imagine if we all knew how to fight well?

When Phil and I were quizzing older couples about how they handled conflict, and all the other things that built their marriage into a strong one, we learned some skills. I was pretty excited to see that Gottman's work exactly reflected this home-spun wisdom, which makes sense when you think about it.

Early on we learned the folly of name-calling, insult-throwing and character-attack.

A lovely lady told me to keep Phil's secrets, and I have. A very elderly couple told us the importance of little affections, so we're always touching each other and we hold hands all the time. We were told, by another wise couple, how important it is to stay in the present in any fight and not sling arrows gathered in previous wars.

Gottman's work has been invaluable to Phil and I because, not only did we learn new ways to do conflict, it helped us understand why and how some of the things we already did worked. And as you already know, I love to know why. Now you'll get to enjoy understanding it too.

Gottman found Magicians handle conflict in an entirely different way to how Muggles do. The difference wasn't that one group had conflict and the other did not, conflict is entirely normal and was common to both. I think it's easy to end up thinking that happy and harmonious relationships are conflict-free relationships. This is not the case.

Magicians get angry just as often as Muggles. They just handle the anger and the conflict differently.

Speaking of conflict, one of the most startling statistics I've read in all of Gottman's work was that 69% of conflict in marriage is over issues that cannot be solved.

Yes, you did read that right, 69% of the conflicts we have with our love partner are about perpetual problems that won't change.

So much for the idea if it's 'true love' everything will be rosy. The things you fight about now will still be unresolved down the track. The difference with Magicians is they know how to fight in a way that doesn't undermine the relationship while the Muggles tend to behave like their partner is the enemy.

It takes some adjusting to, that 69% statistic, don't you think?

AND THAT'S WITH THE ONE YOU LOVE

69%. What really fascinates me about this statistic is you have such a high level of unresolvable differences with the one person you went out and selected from all the other possible 'one persons' in the world! This is with the one you chose!

Imagine the potential for unresolvable issues and ongoing conflicts in all the other relationships you have. It just has to be higher than 69%.

You didn't choose that mother-in-law, that aunt, that father, that child, that sibling, that cousin. Is it any wonder family relationships can be so volatile?

You didn't choose that boss, that co-worker, that bank manager, that school teacher, that choirmaster, or your business partner's wife. Is it any wonder that conflict happens everywhere?

You already know how differently we each see the world and how protective we are of our own view, so the fact we have such a high rate of unresolvable conflict makes perfect sense. Most of our differences can't be remedied.

You won't ever see things as your partner does or ever evolve to have exactly the same taste in music, film or decor.

Or Kitchen buckets.

You have vast differences to your partner and you'll think differently on such basics as how many minutes even equal late; how close you are to your family of origin; and how often you want your mother to stay; how frequently you'd like to have a good heart-to-heart and what activities are fun.

You might be on two ends of the spectrum about exactly what constitutes clean, and what chores need to be done to achieve it. Phil's version of clean is nothing like the version I inherited from my slightly OCD mother.

Often it isn't just a conflict about who has been too lenient with the kids. It's a huge difference in what constitutes leniency in the first place that's the issue. These are things you won't budge on because they're what you believe. The nature of success; your work ethic; and how you spend money are all extremely reliable argument-makers. Then there are straight out simple personality differences.

None of the aforementioned is anything that's going to change anytime soon. Remember I said earlier it's a wonder anyone stays together? This is one of the reasons why I said it.

If you're using your Magician stuff you remember this, and most of the time you don't pressure your people to be someone they're not. This is also an excellent reason to relax about conflicts. They're normal.

However, if you're doing the Muggles-thing, you've moved to a fantasy land where it seems plausible to think that others should change in order to make you happy.

Muggles keep finding others terribly disappointing because they're applying fictional outcomes to reality. Fiction such as, 'If she loves me, she'll agree.'

Remember it's not only your life partner this applies to. Are you furious at your best friend, boss, son-in-law or teacher because they keep behaving like themselves?

And this explains, to a large degree, why you as a Magician, will do conflict very differently to how you handle disagreement if you're being a Muggle. How you decide to do conflict will predict the outcome of your relationships.

IT'S NOT IF YOU FIGHT, IT'S HOW YOU FIGHT

Not rocket science I know. This is what your granny could tell you, yet it's also something I need constant reminders about because the media portrayal of how to do conflict keeps me running back to fantasy land.

If I want to be a Magician I have to work through conflict while causing as little pain as I can. Simple.

Gottman looked at this whole process in great detail and I have him to thank for breaking it down simply enough it can be easily communicated. He even broke it down to four easy-to-remember things.

THE FOUR HORSEMEN OF THE APOCALYPSE

I think Gottman was really a genius to make reference to these dramatic and intimidating names for these four destructive traits. With a name like that, you know immediately these guys are full of drama and will seriously mess up the lounge room if they're allowed to gallop through.

Gottman's four horsemen are criticism, defensiveness, stonewalling and contempt. These traits ride into all relationships, not just marriages, and cause mayhem, misery and miscommunication.

It's important to understand they even ride into relationships that are happy. It's how often you let the riders run amok at your place that separates the Magicians from the Muggles.

THE HORESMEN COMETH

Gottman's work explains clearly the ways these horsemen ride into the fight: In Gottman's great book *'The 7 Principles For Making Marriage Work'* he looks at this process in great detail. Here's a quick run down.

Criticism: If you're riding toward disaster and being a Muggle then you'll resort to criticism and blame the other person for the problem. You'll see yourself as the victim of their actions.

You'll hear yourself say things like 'Well if you hadn't done ...' or 'This is typical of you'. You might get sarcastic and you won't accept any responsibility for the issue at hand. You'll be doing some serious finger pointing and you'll be expecting the other person to change. You won't see yourself as part of the problem.

Actually, deep down, you may well feel the other person should thank you for the wisdom you've imparted to them.

Magicians do a lot of tongue biting. Sometimes their tongues bleed.

Magicians avoid Criticism: When you take responsibility for at least some of the problem, communicate your feelings gently, being careful not to hurt their feelings, or belittle them, and don't give into that desire to air your resentments, or criticise the other person then you get to be the Magician.

Defensiveness: If you 'Muggle It', you're immediately self-protective, closed and defensive. You whine, play the innocent victim and launch straight in with a counter attack when any issue is raised. You may barely give the other person a chance to finish what they're saying before you get into battle mode. You know you're getting defensive when you can hear yourself say things like 'Well that's nothing compared to what you do…' or 'Yeah, but what about you, you never…'

Magicians remain open and vulnerable: While your Downstairs Brain is screaming for you to get defensive you decide to stay open and vulnerable if you've got the Magician hat on. You really want to see this situation improve so you ask how you've contributed to the problem. Even when an issue is first raised, you respond with interest and seek information instead of becoming defensive.

Rather than letting loose all the emotions that start to bubble up, you stay calm or take a break if you feel a bit of Downstairs coming on. You work against your natural desire to defend.

Stonewalling: If you're a Muggle drama queen you're probably using some dramatic stonewalling devices such as sulking. If you're stonewalling, you'll be walking out of the room in a huff and slamming doors. Locking the door, refusing to open the door and refraining from communication, is a very Mugglish way to handle things. When an issue is raised, as a stonewalling Muggle, you'll often refuse to engage right from the start and you're frequently dismissive of the concerns of the other person. If you hear yourself saying things like 'Don't be ridiculous…' or 'Give me a break, that's what's worrying you?' or 'I don't want to talk about it.' or 'You're just too sensitive,' then you'll know you've Muggled off to stonewalling. Interestingly, according to Dr Gottman, 85% of stonewallers in heterosexual relationship are men.

Magicians engage and listen: Magicians are happy the other person values the relationship enough to work things out. They listen and try to understand where the other person is coming from. Magicians try to see it from the other person's point of view and are patient, allowing the person to get it all out. They're not planning their own argument and mentally ticking off points to counter. They're listening and staying engaged.

Magicians know far from being an uncomfortable inconvenience, it is a wonderful thing someone in the world values you enough to actually want to work out a problem with you. Magicians engage where Muggles dis-engage.

Contempt: When you behave in an arrogant manner, when you think you know better, when you start name-calling, look out! Contempt has galloped in and you're being a Muggle. When you act out of contempt, you can become cruel, throwing accusations and saying things that demean the character of the other person. You've got to the point where you really believe you are the superior one. You roll your eyes, correct the other person and behave in a mean and disrespectful manner when you've invited the dark horseman of contempt into your relationship.

Magicians Are Respectful: As a Magician you treat the other person with respect find ways to allow them to maintain their dignity. Even when you are angry you refrain from any sort of put-down. You stay kind, even when tempted to be otherwise. At the end of the conflict the other person still feels valued.

If you recognise contempt as playing a role in your relationships and you'd like things to change then I suggest you pay particular attention to the final chapter of this book, you'll be needing some Love Potion.

In the end a lot of this hinges on our decision to be respectful or not. Respect is the opposite of contempt and contempt is a fatal cancer for a relationship. Gottman maintains contempt is the biggest predictor of relationship break down.

A SULKY PRINCESS

Stonewalling was something I was excellent at. I'd sulk for days, walk out of the room when things got heated and I was quite accomplished at door slamming. It wasn't until I read Gottman's work that I twigged how aggressive, bullying and horrible it is to stonewall. Here was I thinking I was the poor one, so hard done-by, when really I was the one controlling the shots, not allowing others to even finish what they were saying and refusing to communicate until I got my way. Sulking, silent treatment and all that goes with it, is awful, manipulative and selfish.

Leaving people without explanations, or without the opportunity to be heard is just plain cruel and extremely controlling behaviour. Dismissing the concerns of another person just because they aren't your concerns is arrogant and thoughtless. Yes, I was such a peach.

These days I make a much bigger effort to listen. Even if I'm not particularly concerned about the issue myself, I want to let the other person be heard and I want to be considerate enough to attempt to understand them, even when it gets uncomfortable.

I'm not saying leaving a conversation when it gets heated is a bad thing. It's not. Often it's the wisest thing you could do. I'm just saying leaving in a way that further inflames things isn't going to help.

Phil and I both agree that to go to bed angry or to have some time out when things get too emotional is our best bet for productive fighting.

'Okay darling, I need to leave the room now before I say something I won't really mean. We'll get back to this,' is very different to saying 'I can't stand this!' and storming out the door.

YOU CAN BE BOTH ON ANY GIVEN DAY

One of the important things to understand about Magicians and Muggles is we're not locked into either group.

Being human, both Magicians and Muggles will get things wrong. When I'm talking about Magician behaviour, and Gottman's research about how his Master Magicians respond in a fight, I'm meaning 'most of the time'. Sometimes I'll be a Magician and sometimes I'll behave like a Muggle.

The key is the more frequently I choose the craft, the practice of love, the happier all my relationships are.

Fighting fair is crucial to the survival of your relationships.

Gottman has written widely and well on this subject and his website has some great resources too. The next chapter is all about words and will fit snugly with the content of this one.

PRACTICE

Remind Yourself Often That People Are Precious

There is only one of each person. Utterly unique, special, incredible, amazing, and, yes, they can often be annoying too. Remind yourself that they're here in your life for a reason. You don't want to miss out on the contribution they alone can make to your life. They're precious, and there will never be another quite like them.

‘Attention is the rarest and purest form of generosity.’

SIMONE WEIL

12

ATTENTION PLEASE

Phil and I have spent most of our married life working at home or in situations that meant we were very available to our kids. It's been important to us they felt secure. I've always been a tad 'helicopter' as a parent. I'm quite good at imagining the worst case scenario. Fortunately Phil's been a good balance for my anxious approach. I doubt he spent a minute considering the perils of having a backyard flying fox or what could possibly go wrong taking the kids rock fishing. His parenting is of the laid-back, free-range style.

'Kids? What Kids? Don't you have them?' was his reply on more than one occasion when I'd left him babysitting.

Looking back I see my fears often took control to a degree that probably didn't make my children feel secure at all. And these fears also affected the way I communicated with them.

When I was researching relationships some years ago, I came across an interesting study by psychological researcher Shelly Gable. Reading her findings gave me a very serious 'aha' moment.

I realised I'd often, in the name of helping and protecting, put the damper on my children's great ideas and dreams. Sometimes I was even stealing the joy from their good news.

Some years ago our youngest daughter was telling us about her plans to open a pub with her boyfriend and a few other friends. These weren't actual 'happening anytime soon' plans, just an idea they were forming, one they cared about. I gave them everything I had.

'Oh God, you don't want to go into business with friends, that's a bad idea, it never works. It'll end in tears. And a pub? A pub? Are you mad? Pubs are crazy expensive to set up. Have you looked at the cost of a liquor license? And they're not something you can count on, you can lose them, they can be revoked, then what do you have? There are stacks of pubs. There must be better options you could look at. And you, are you sure you want to run a business? Have you thought about this? You're not someone I think of as having the drive it takes to run a business. You do know you never get a single day off when you run your own business don't you? Never. Not a day. It's crazy, it'll drive you crazy. And what if you break up with your boyfriend? What happens then? You'll lose all your money...'

I remember that conversation now and cringe. What an awful thing to do to her dream. In my mind I'm helping her look at the situation realistically because she's young and I'm afraid she'll get hurt or lose money. However, she hadn't asked me for advice. She'd only shared a dream and instead of encouraging her to look forward with hope, I sucked the life out of her. I also burdened her with fears she didn't need and that don't contribute to her sense of security. It was insensitive and thoughtless. I hate to think how many times I've done this to our kids.

and everyone I know!

As you can see I'm great at seeing problems. It's my gift and my curse.

This gift allows me to run beautiful events where almost nothing ever goes wrong because I've already thought of every potential problem. This gift allows me to make sure I have everything I need for a trip. I'm the one with the band-aids, spare coat, pillows, the hip flask of gin and enough candles for 30 blackouts.

I get ribbed about my over-planning all the time and I easily recognise how crazy I'm being. Sometimes though my friends have also have had good reason to be happy I'm like this, such as when they're travelling with me and need some candles or gin.

However this is a gift with many disadvantages. Downsides that include catastrophising, complaining, being a fussy customer and, sadly, the overwhelming need to protect others from possible problems.

As if I could and as if that's good. Duh!

ROCKS AHEAD?

Do you know the boat scene in the film *The Princess Bride?* If you do you're smiling now because that film has the best lines ever written and many of them happen in the boat. Inigo Montoya (a wandering swordsman out to avenge his father's death) asks the giant Fezzik (a soft but deadly teddy bear) 'Are there rocks ahead?' and Fezzik, answers, 'If there are, we'll all be dead'.

I'm the Fezzik in the room and I don't even wait for people to ask if there are rocks ahead. I stand at the helm of the boat and yell 'Watch out! There are rocks ahead, we'll all be dead!'

This is the only film I've watched more than 50 times. Fans of the film tend to get a little addicted to it.

RESPONSE TO GOOD NEWS

In 2006 Shelly Gable did a wonderful study on how couples respond to good news. Again, it was couple research that gave me insight and allowed me to understand better the effect of my behaviour on people in general, not just in my marriage. Gable's work is unusual because, while a lot of research looks at problems, Gable looked at something positive, the communication of good news.

People respond to good news in one of four ways:

> **1. Active Destructive:** Vocally and enthusiastically negative, pointing out problems, possibly sarcastic.

2. Passive Destructive: Non-responsive, uncommunicative, negative, not listening, muttering under breath.

3. Passive Constructive: Supportive but not communicative, slightly positive yet impassive or distracted.

4. Active Constructive: Communicative, supportive, validating, displays pleasure, shows support, asks questions, is interested.

In the experiment, Gable had couples tell each other a piece of good news such as 'Hey, I got into med school!' and then each of their responses was noted and assigned to one of the four categories.

ACTIVE CONSTRUCTIVE OUTCOMES

Some months after the interviews, Gable's team followed up with the couples to see how they were getting along and if they were still together. She found those couples where the partner responded in an 'Active Constructive' manner had better relationship outcomes compared to those who responded in any of the other three styles. These 'Active Constructive' couples had higher relationship quality, increased intimacy and they tended to still be together.

When reading Gable's work I realised that often my response to someone's good news or great idea was 'Active Destructive', the worst possible response. Even though my intention was to help, I'd be vocal about negatives and point out the downside. While I wasn't sarcastic, I certainly wasn't doling out the generosity.

My lovely daughter-in-law Hannah read the proof copy of this book and said she didn't agree with my assessment of myself being frequently 'Active Destructive'. She says I've always been enthusiastic and supportive to her. Who knew? I was very relieved to hear that I'm not awful all the time.

FRANCE ANYONE?

Life is pretty exciting at the moment for Phil and I. We're about to travel to Europe! I'm especially excited because we'll be going to Paris. I've been dreaming about Paris since I was 16. Once I was so close I could almost touch it. I was in London and it was only a train trip away and I very, very, very nearly jumped on that train. Yet, when I thought about going to Paris without Phil, I suddenly didn't want to go anymore. I'd just been in Oxford alone and found being unable to share the sights with him reduced the enjoyment dramatically. No worries though, I'll take him to Oxford in a few weeks.

So we've got good news to tell and I've been telling everyone!

I thought it might be a helpful illustration of these four styles of responding if I put them in the context of our trip to Paris. I've given you four possible responses you might have when I tell you my good news.

'Guess what? We're finally going to France!'

Active Destructive: 'France? Now? There's so much terrorism, I don't think it's safe. Anyway you don't speak French and the French will be rude to you if you don't speak their language. And the railway stations, they're very dangerous these days. My aunt told me they're full of homeless refugees and pickpockets. She said it was very scary.'

> It's true, I don't speak French. However I already knew that. I was planning to learn it this week and somehow managed not to. Your 'Active Destructive' response only adds to my anxiety and I'm already anxious enough. I'm the worrywart of all worrywarts. This answer indicates you think I haven't thought this through or I'm not very smart.

← This isn't what I want to hear!

Passive Destructive: 'Ok, well you won't believe what happened to me. I got pulled over by a cop yesterday.'

If you think I'll tell you about seeing Van Morrison play in Northern Ireland you've got another think coming.

> You ignored my good news! Then you countered with other news effectively making mine null. Thanks a lot! While not overtly negative this reply is destructive because I feel dismissed, ignored and unheard. Something that is so huge for me isn't even worthy of acknowledgement.

Passive Constructive: 'Oh yeah? That's great.'

> As a response this one sounds okay, however you didn't make eye contact with me and then you pulled out your phone to start texting while I was adding more details! Rude. Your response is half-hearted, understated and doesn't show any real interest in me or my news. Again, I feel dismissed and unimportant.

Active Constructive: 'Oh you're kidding! I'm so pleased, that's great news, finally! You've been talking about going to Paris forever. What happened, how did you decide, where are you going? Tell me all about it. Are you doing Airbnb? That's so exciting, you'll have a ball!'

> Your 'Active Constructive' response is wholehearted, excited and vocal. You joined me in my excitement, showed interest and, above all, have given me your undivided attention. I feel cared for. Being invited to share the details of my trip with someone is very special. I get added enjoyment out of my travel plans when I can talk about them with you. I feel like kissing your feet. I'll definitely tell you that Van Morrison is playing at a dinner with only about 298 other people attending because you'll be excited for me.

Only the final one, 'Active Constructive', is kind. Only 'Active Constructive' lets people know they matter and only the 'Active Constructive' is a joy-making relationship builder.

TAPPING INTO JOY

When you give 'Active Constructive' responses to ideas and to good news you let people know that you see them. They know you care, they know they matter and they know that, somewhere in the world, there is someone who will rejoice with them.

When you respond positively to good news and ideas you get a big bonus because you get to experience the joy another person feels.

If you really want to make someone else feel great, then get them to tell you their good news story again. Be deliberate. Request more detail, allow them to shine.

Many of our achievements are hard-won and the work that goes into them is unseen. Allow others to boast, allow them to revel in their achievement of the good thing that is happening. Giving your friend or family member the opportunity to tell another human all about their news or achievement is a rare gift. One they'll love you for and one that will bring both of you joy. I'm learning to make this the way I respond to good news and new ideas.

Sharing joy, sharing positive moments, laughing together and having meaningful experiences together bonds relationships.

This is another thing that you already know, yet are you taking time to make sure it's happening?

Oh God, look who is talking! This is exactly what I haven't been doing the past few years. I'm glad I wrote a book and reminded myself. I haven't been making the time for those joyous, positive shared experiences with my family and I'm publicly committing, now, to making that a priority.

SOME FRIENDS ARE SO FRIENDLY

When Phil and I have good news there are some people we can't wait to tell because they get excited and celebrate with us. What you really want when you share good news is some effervescence, some good energy, a bit of 'Whoo hoo!'

We have some friends who are so excited by our good news, it's as though it happened to them. They ask us questions, let us relive it and often their interest even continues after the initial telling. Sometimes they'll call to see how whatever we've shared is progressing. This keeps the joy going. We get to feel like rock stars when we share good news with those friends and we're really lucky to have people in our lives who display this sort of generosity toward us.

SOME FRIENDS ARE NOT SO FRIENDLY

Over the years some friendships have waned and looking back we can see the friendships that haven't stood the test of time were often with people who were unable to be happy for us or take joy in our achievements.

One female friend in particular was constantly passive aggressive. She'd throw little pins into the conversation and, while Phil wouldn't notice her jabs, I'd reel back in shock. Her aggression was so subtle I couldn't really put my finger on what it actually was she'd said that left me feeling like I'd been put down. After a conversation with her I'd talk about it to Phil and my older kids trying to work out what was going on. Was I imagining this?

One day the jab was so clear I knew I hadn't been imagining things.

I'd started a Uni course when I was 40 and was learning to draw. I'd always wanted to draw yet had been told in high school not to pursue art as a subject because I had no talent.

Oh the power of words, especially when they come from a teacher.

When I started this course, I had so many insecurities about my artistic potential I almost pulled out. Fortunately I was lucky enough to have an incredible teacher who taught technique and, very quickly, I began to improve. I was so excited about my progress, I could barely believe what I was producing.

One day the aforementioned friend, an accomplished artist herself, was visiting and I proudly showed her my drawings.

Her 'Active Destructive' comment was along the lines of 'I wonder if you'll feel so excited about these drawings when you've learned a bit more'. She looked at me with pity. I felt totally put down.

She was completely unable to encourage, share or be generous in a moment that was very exciting for me. This was one of the friendships that eventually petered out.

KINDNESS IS UNDERRATED

Kindness is totally underrated. People can't get enough of it. It doesn't matter if it's your workplace, within your family or with your friends, kindness is the key. I don't want the big gestures, I don't crave being wined and dined by Phil, or taken on weekends away.

Well except to Paris. Did I happen to mention we're going to Paris?

I don't want him to buy me a car, or jewellery or any fine thing. I have no need of any of that because every day he is constantly, unfailingly kind to me. He's a Magician and Magicians know a lot about kindness. Muggles, sadly, think it's optional.

Kindness is the car that love travels in.

PICK ME!

Do you remember being a kid in school with your hand up? You're sitting there dying for the teacher to notice you. 'Me Miss, me, pick me.' You wave your hand, you try to get your arm to go higher and if the teacher is taking a while you might need to use your other arm to hold the raised one up.

You're still that child. You and I, we're still that child needing to be noticed, needing to be the one that is chosen, needing to be heard. We just have new, more adult ways, of asking for that attention.

We're so cute, all just little kids waving our hands wanting to be noticed.

BIDDING FOR ATTENTION

Dr Gottman, the man with the gadgets and jiggleometers from the last chapter, talks about this 'hand-raising' a lot. He calls it Bids for Attention. It reminds me of Shelly Gable's 'Active Constructive' work, so this is why they're sharing a chapter together. I thought they'd get on with each other.

Gottman describes how we're all making constant bids for attention and he maintains that how others respond to those bids will either build or destroy trust. And I think that's true of 'Active Constructive' responses. I know I'm with someone I can trust, who has my back, if they can get in my space and celebrate my wins.

As an adult, the sort of bids you make will vary. Many are tiny, so small our friends and family can easily ignore them. You may not be aware you're even making them. You make them when you ask your partner to tell you about their day and you make one when you show a co-worker a video on YouTube. When you point out beautiful scenery to a friend you're making a bid for their attention just as you are when you tell your mum a story about what happened at the gym.

It's always wise to be aware of little things. Termites are little things but if you ignore them you'll find either a massive bill or a house that falls down.

So it is with bids for attention, ignore them at your peril.

THE TURNS

Gottman observes there are three typical responses to bids for attention: Turning toward, turning away, and turning against.

Turning Toward: When your partner responds to your query about their day with, 'Not bad, I'll grab a drink and tell you about it.' They've turned toward you. Magician!

Turning Away: When they respond with, 'I'm tired, I don't want to talk about it.' They've turned away from you. Aww, Muggle.

Turning Against: If they respond with, 'I'm really tired! Just leave me alone, you're always hassling me.' They've very effectively turned against you. Cranky Muggle.

These last two responses will, according to Gottman, decrease your trust a little each time you encounter them. When you make a bid for attention and people regularly turn 'away' or 'against' you lose heart and make fewer bids. You'll raise your hand less and less.

Gottman's statistics indicate you have to turn toward a bid eight or nine times out of 10 to keep trust strong. If you only turn once or twice out of every 10 opportunities the chances you'll damage the relationship, in time, are high.

This is because the bid for attention is asking a very big and very important question, 'Do I matter to you?'

DO I MATTER TO YOU?

When your kids, parents, friends or partners make a bid for attention they are really asking you, 'Do I matter to you?'

This has been so important for me to learn. Again, it's simple stuff I already knew was good for relationships, I just didn't understand why it was so good. When Gottman explained how trust is destroyed I could see why a positive response to bids was essential. Now I'm much more aware of exactly what my children, grandchildren and friends are asking me when they want me to watch a YouTube video or show me their drawings.

This could mean you have to watch a lot of YouTube videos

HANDS DOWN

When someone repeatedly turns away or turns against your bids for attention you learn to keep your hand down. They don't see you, you go unnoticed and that hurts the first time, and the second, and the third and every single time after. Being ignored tells you clearly you don't really matter to this person. You can't trust that person to be kind to you and deep down this hurt will foster great resentment.

> Relationships flounder on the smallest things, the build-up of little rejections, the tiny erosions of trust, the absence of the little kindnesses.

It isn't always easy or convenient to turn toward a bid for attention. You're busy and the interruptions to your day these bids bring, can be frustrating or annoying. However, kindness, kindness, kindness is what you constantly have to bring to the table if you want to enjoy good relationships and get the magic happening.

FUN OR FANGS?

Teasing has always been a big deal in our household. Phil loves to tease. Somehow, in the area of teasing, most of our kids took after their dad. They didn't get their more extreme teasing genes from me. I like playful, affectionate teasing, it's bonding. However the kind that creates amusement for one person, or a crowd, at the expense of another, I find emotionally wearing, embarrassing and ultimately, unkind.

Certain people in my family used to find it funny to see me panic because of what they'd said, 'Oh my God, so and so just had a terrible accident', or find joy in telling me the wrong time just to see me get stressed about being late. I'd end up feeling stupid to have, yet again, fallen for their 'jokes'. When I say 'used to', it's because I had to ask them to stop teasing me, which they kindly did. They're all rather nice. I just couldn't take the emotional roller-coaster that even their reasonably friendly teasing created for me. I've got enough of my own anxieties and stresses, both real and imagined, without dealing with someone else's created ones. Also, years and years of feeling stupid, does nothing for a person.

I wanted to bring teasing up because teasing is a form of 'bids for attention' that can backfire rather badly. I also wanted to point out when I'm talking about Phil and I laughing together and, in chapter two, finding each other's faults a source of endless amusement, I'm not necessarily talking about teasing. If it's kind, and affectionate then bring it on, however teasing can quickly turn into all sorts of other things:

> *'Teasing is central to human social life. People tease to socialize, flirt, resolve conflicts, and pass the time in imaginative and playful ways. With slight variations in utterance and display, teasing can lead to more disturbing ends, as when teasing humiliates or harasses. Teasing is often subsumed under, and at times conflated with, humor, play, irony, sarcasm, and bullying.'*

From '*Just Teasing: A Conceptual Analysis and Empirical Review 2001 Psychological Bulletin.*'

Australians are big teasers, it's a very common way we relate and I love the relaxed atmosphere teasing can create. Teasing can get you a lot of attention and can also create serious damage to relationships, especially if it's done publicly, when it's used like this:

To raise a personal emotional issue

To point out faults in your partner/friend

To gain support for your stance

To attack someone's character

To humiliate someone

To put someone down

To expose a secret

To show contempt

To bully someone

Couples, even friends, will often raise painful issues, or point to some problem the other person has through publicly teasing the person. Effectively they're saying 'Oh hey, look over here everyone, pay attention to my friend's faults'. The teasing might be done with lots of laughing and joking yet the effects can be anything but funny. You've pointed out a weakness in public, you've drawn attention to it. Those witnessing the exchange will feel the venom and feel uncomfortable. The person who's been the target of any of the above will feel betrayed, hurt and angry.

'Oh, I was just teasing. I didn't mean anything' is one way to both put someone down and let yourself off the hook when you've been passive aggressive.

If the teasing is 'against' someone, rather than 'toward', it probably isn't going to serve your relationship.

The next chapter will be about words, another great way to show kindness.

PS: Van Morrison was incredible!

PRACTICE

Take A Minute

If, day-in and day-out, you take just that one extra minute to be interested, to watch that video, agree the scenery is stunning, and answer the question with patience, you'll build huge reservoirs of trust. You've let your people know they matter to you. As Simone Weil said so well at the beginning of this chapter:

'Attention is the rarest and purest form of generosity.'

Put the phone away and look them in the eye.

'Words are
seeds that do more than
blow around. They land in
our hearts and not the ground.
Be careful what you plant and
careful what you say.
You might have to eat
what you planted
one day.'

UNKNOWN

13

THE POWER OF WORDS

I've had some amazingly good advice in my life, the brutal words of wisdom from Donna for a start. One piece of stellar advice was from an older woman and I'm devoting a whole chapter to it, it's that good.

Very early in our marriage I was at a luncheon where a woman was speaking about relationships. I don't remember her name, however I can still clearly recall the significant things she said. Her powerful words, two short sentences, are burned into my memory and, to this day, are still affecting my life. The first was:

> *'People can be created or destroyed by words, the words you say about others will influence who they become.'*

Then she added the killer line, 'Fidelity is not just sexual. Faithfulness is having your partner's back in all that you say about them.'

I know she conveyed this message very clearly to me; the words I said to others about Phil, either behind his back, or more importantly, in his hearing, would affect him. I could say words he'd rise up to or I could say words that would cut him down. My words would contribute to how he saw himself and my words would help shape, in time, who he would become. I'll come back to her words shortly.

MARRIAGE

When first we were married we lived in public housing. Phil rode his beloved pushbike to work in frigid Canberra winters and earned just $75 a week.

There was no joyous 'mummy-to-be' in our small flat. I wasn't buying baby clothes or choosing prams. I was more occupied with trying to work out how I'd cope with this baby's terrible imagined disabilities or how one organised a funeral for a newborn. I'd been watching way too much TV and had seen what seemed like a non-stop run of scary ads telling me 'One in every 10 babies has a disability'. I was sure I'd met at least 10 babies that looked normal and I'd become convinced our baby would be dead, or at the least, terribly deformed. I didn't buy any baby things. We didn't settle a name. I didn't want to buy a cot because I couldn't even imagine this baby would ever really come home to live with us.

There is that slight, tendency to catastrophise again!

Instead of picking baby things I wanted to pick fights.

I was afraid, the future seemed uncertain. Could I even handle suburban life let alone motherhood? What on earth did we think we were doing?

He'd arrive home each night to my chaos, both internal and external. He'd see the sink full of dirty dishes and say 'You cleaned the toilet! You're amazing.' He noticed what little I did do and ignored the rest.

Over the years his generous words kept coming always affirming what was good about me, what was hopeful. He always saw the potential I had, he always affirmed who I could be. Every time I'd try to fight with him, Phil would just laugh and kiss me till I smiled.

Even I found it hard to argue with grace.

THEY WERE AFRAID

When I think back to all the people who opposed our marriage, I see they were afraid I would break him, that my anger would be his undoing. I think they were right to be afraid. He was a gentle man and I did have, ready to roll, every weapon I needed to destroy him.

I had rage. I had fear, buckets of it. I had insecurity, criticism, contempt all wrapped up in a blanket of selfishness and I was a girl careless with my words. All these are things that make a person vulnerable to pointing the finger, laying blame and finding fault. And I think I would have often done just that just to feel a little better about me. I think it's often why we do run someone down, we feel so bad about ourselves.

Had it not been for that unknown woman's timely words so early on, I think I would have, unthinkingly, done just that. Her wise words rang like a bell in my mind, and have rung year in and year out, reminding me to be careful with this treasure. Reminding me not to destroy a beautiful man.

It's all too easy to ruin a relationship or destroy a person, with a few ill-chosen words.

REPAIRED

For 40 years, Phil has been relentless in his flow of kind words, despite my offering him many reasons to be critical. This isn't because he's stupid. He's not blind. He sees my faults. He's aware of all of them, and yet, he has never battered me with his words.

He has instead, in tiny acts of stunning grace, repaired me with them.

I MARRIED AN ANGEL

All this may make Phil sound like he's perfect. Hilariously someone said to me the other day, 'You know, don't you, if you publish this book someone is going to knock you off so they can have Phil?' I laughed and laughed.

If this is your plan then please be aware while he'll overlook a lot of crap he's probably not going to overlook murder.

He is great, however, he isn't perfect. He can be all sorts of annoying, and even has his own set of faults.

It was only last year, on an early morning car trip, that I leaned toward him and said, not unkindly, 'Darling, I just want to let you know that right now, at this moment, I'd dearly love to kill you.'

He smiled, however he knew what I was talking about and knew I was letting him know we had stuff to sort out.

What ended up being funny about making this particular comment on that particular day is we were on the way to a day-long relationship workshop we were holding. As I was about to speak about having happier relationships I had to confess my comment to the whole room in order to run the workshop with any integrity.

So he's not perfect, however, for the most part, people don't hear much about his faults from me. Though, as I did mention them to you just now, I'll have to swear you to secrecy, okay?

I mostly tell people this about him, 'I married an angel, he's amazing. He's one of the world's nicest people'. And he is, that's who he is.

SCARY POWER

Words have scary power. Just one word from me about another person can influence what you understand about, and how you interpret the behaviour of the person I've mentioned. It's how your brain works. You sieve the information coming in through the grid of what you already know. Your brain will set up a bias depending on what it has already heard.

If you hear the new girl at work is a bitch then, possibly ever after, you'll see a bitch. You're more likely to ascribe bitchy motives to the things she does. Let's imagine though she isn't a bitch and the bit of nastiness you heard came from someone who is jealous of her. In time you might get to know this girl and you might discover she's a very kind person.

However, you might not ever get to know her because of a few poison words that set up a bias against her. Our words have great power, they'll affect who people perceive someone to be.

WORDS AFFECT OTHERS

Phil and I experienced bias when we moved to the small town where we ran the festival. The thing about small towns is word travels fast. The power of bias was one of the things that generated some huge questions in me.

Very early on a well-known local somehow decided I'd created the festival for power and personal gain, an opinion she shared with others. She was a prominent person in that small community and her opinion was respected. The entire four years I worked on the festival I continually bumped up against this rumour, which didn't make my job any easier.

I was totally perplexed, nothing we said to refute this impression made any difference at all. Telling people we'd worked 10 years as full-time volunteers, didn't shift their opinion. Telling people we'd once sold our only home and, after repaying our debt and buying a car, had given the rest of the money to charity fell on deaf ears. The fact we'd almost never made a decision based on monetary benefits to ourselves, something any fool could see if they looked, was fruitless. Even the fact almost all not-for-profit events are only able to run because volunteers give their time and key people work for no or low wages, made no difference to their thinking.

The situation seemed, unbelievably, to suggest to us that facts don't matter at all if people have formed their opinions. It turns out that's the truth. In the face of bias, facts don't matter at all.

Now I know more about naive realism, blind spots and how our brains sieve information to confirm what we already believe, what we encountered now makes sense to me. You'll recall that this sieving is called 'confirmation bias'.

THE SORT OF PERSON YOU SEE

One of the things that happens, if you regularly speak ill of your partner or friends, is your brain will become attentive to their faults. You're telling your brain their faults are quite interesting and your brain thinks, 'Cool, let's have another look at these interesting thoughts'. You'll notice more faults and those faults will become annoying.

Quite soon it might be their faults are all you are noticing about them.

The opposite will be true if you begin to take note of their good qualities.

In 2012, I was doing a workshop with the staff of a charity. At morning tea a woman came up to me and told me she was planning to divorce her husband. Naturally I was curious and asked her to tell me about it. 'Oh he's nice, he's a nice guy. There's nothing wrong with him. It's just that I don't love him. I'm bored and I want to move on. This is going nowhere.' I could see there was still so much hope for this couple, so I asked her to try something before she went ahead with plans for divorce.

What I asked her to try was this, 'For the next 30 days pay attention to all his good qualities. Notice what he does for you, notice what he does well, notice what he does for others. Look out for every single thing you can find that is good about him. At least once a day give him a genuine compliment and at least once a day thank him.' I finished up by giving her my number and asking her to call me at the end of the 30 days. Then I went home and forgot all about it.

Thirty days later I got a call from this lady. The very first thing she said was 'I am so in love with him'.

Even I hadn't expected that good an outcome.

It was an incredible story. One I told at workshops for the next few years. Then one day I thought to myself, 'You know, this story is a little bit too good to be true, are you sure it happened? You don't even know her name. Did she actually ring or did youadd that bit?' I couldn't be sure, I didn't actually know her name and because I couldn't verify the story I stopped telling it.

In November 2015 I was running a workshop in Brisbane and using the brand new premises of the same charity I'd done the workshop for three years prior. A woman came up to me at morning tea, 'You won't remember me,' she began, 'but I talked to you three years ago.'

It was her! She proceeded to tell me the exact same story I'd told so many times. In fact she was now telling me three years down the track she was still happily married to the man she loved so much! It was an incredible story she went on to share with the whole room later in the day.

In a bit of super serendipity, just today, as I was editing this chapter the same woman emailed me out of the blue. It's the first time I've heard from her since she addressed the workshop that day in 2015. She finished her email with: 'Yes, we're still together and all is good in our world'. I emailed back and told her I was using her story in my book and she was thrilled.

Fairly recently I read a fabulous book about stories and the power of what we say called *'Broadcasting Happiness'* by Michelle Gielan. This is an excellent read if you're interested in understanding the power you are wielding in your own life and the lives of others, when you speak. This quote from Michelle illustrates why criticising others isn't helpful to them:

> *'People are pulled towards the best in themselves, and spotlighting the right is a much stronger approach than nagging.'*

The words you use about your family, partner, friends and co-workers are also profoundly influencing them. Those words also influence who you perceive the person to be and how you interpret their behaviour.

WORDS AFFECT WHO YOU BECOME

Words won't only affect the outcome of the lives of others, they'll affect your life. Knowing I was writing about words, a friend kindly started looking for a favourite Buddhist quote that turned out to be not as Buddhist as she'd first thought. The quote seems to have been said by Frank Outlaw, late President of Bi-Lo.

'Watch your thoughts, they become words; Watch your words, they become actions; Watch your actions they become habits; Watch your habits, they become character; Watch your character, for it becomes your destiny.'

THE SKILL OF KINDNESS

Did you know that kindness is a skill? A skill you can develop and the more frequently you are kind the more often you'll actually want to be kind.

Little tiny practices pay great big dividends especially in relationships. Start speaking more kindly, even when you're upset and you're very likely to find big shifts happening.

This is Kind of wonderful don't you think?

Start saying kind things about others, rather than your criticisms, and you'll find you like those people more. Start focusing, as Phil did for me, on what your kids, parents, relatives, partners and boss do well, and you'll find you enjoy those people more. They'll probably enjoy you more too. What you may even find is those people start feeling good about themselves and when you feel good about yourself, you're way less likely to act in petulant, reactive and selfish ways.

Every day you have to make the choice about how you'll use your words. Batter or Repair? One will create freedom for your relationships to grow, and the other will put more bricks in the wall between you.

AND A LITTLE CAVEAT

Words are an influence not a magic potion. Just saying kind words about a mean person probably won't change them. You have to speak the truth, not make stuff up.

For instance talking up the good points of certain people could all backfire badly. Imagine if you were in a marriage with someone who you're afraid of, maybe someone who is abusive and yet you always tell everyone how great they are. No one knows about the other stuff because you've been so positive.

In your mind you're doing what I said was good for the person's growth and you hope it will somehow contribute to their transformation. However, with this person the bad points may hugely outweigh the good ones and in time your fears are realised.

The fall-out from your kindness could have implications in court, implications with friends, implications with relatives. Who can back your story if no one knows what is going on?

Please be careful with this advice. If you're afraid of someone don't go around telling everyone they're fabulous. Get some help.

KEEPING IT PRIVATE

One of Phil and my main rules when sorting out our problems has been to sort them out in private. I don't want to shame him, he doesn't want to shame me. Being confronted with your faults and working through emotional issues is uncomfortable at the best of times, to make it more uncomfortable and add shame into the mix isn't going to help the outcome.

The main issue for both Very Nice and Cruella, in chapter three, was the very public way the conflict was handled. They both felt humiliated. None of us enjoy being corrected or confronted in front of others because we feel embarrassed. Yet, look around, adults frequently bring up personal issues, resentments and the like in front of others. Even in front of strangers.

I've done it myself in a joking, passive-aggressive way and even that is hurtful and humiliating to those on the receiving end.

If you take up an issue with someone publicly, even in a teasing or joking way, you damage the trust in the relationship. That person now knows you don't really have their back. Maybe that friend or family member won't want to be with you when others are present, because they feel unsafe with you and they're afraid the same thing will happen.

BETWEEN OURSELVES

In general, I think it's a great rule to keep the conflict as much between the two parties as possible. However, I also feel ridiculous writing this because on this very thing I haven't done well. In general, with Phil, I'm pretty good. I take the issues to him rather than to others and mostly no one knows about them. Fine.

I've always espoused that we, as humans, should take our stuff to the person involved and that's the way I prefer things to be happening. However, when I can't talk directly to the person involved because they prefer not to discuss it or I'm pretty sure they'll explode, then I tend to vent about it to others. This isn't a great trait and I'm working on ways to handle myself better in these situations.

Again, I don't mean keep it private if it's a situation that is, in any way, abusive or where you feel threatened.

THE STORIES WE TELL

Stories. You string together a bunch of words and use them to explain yourself to others. Maybe sometimes you use your stories to amuse, sometimes you might use them to avoid responsibility, and sometimes you might use them to annihilate someone.

Other times you'll tell yourself sad, bad stories, about the people who did you wrong and you'll provide yourself with very satisfying evidence for why you're not happy. If you're like me you'll run these stories again and again.

Individual words are powerful, stories are possibly even more so.

Hopefully, as you've read some of the preceding chapters you'll now know, if you didn't already know, a lot of our stories are quite fictional. They're designed, albeit unconsciously, to protect ourselves from ourselves.

HOW I RUINED FOUR YEARS

Sometimes you may even allow the 'bad' in your life to become such a focus it actually obliterates the memory of the 'good' happening now or the 'good' in your past.

This is exactly what I did when the film festival ended badly. From the moment I read that email my life went into an emotional tail-spin of panic, shock, hurt, and utter bewilderment. I struggled with a range of emotions that took me on a wild and dangerous ride. One minute I'd be in a rage, the next scared, the next ashamed.

In time, as I focused on all that was happening and watched the effects cascade, very unfairly I thought, through my life, I developed some negative associations with anything to do with the festival. Even someone saying the name of the town or of the event shot pain through my mind and body.

I began to associate the festival and the whole four years with failure, pain, loss and, at least imagined, betrayal. Eventually I had no good memories of that time, it was all regret and wild rage. In my mind I created a tale about a stupid &^%%ing town, I regretted starting that stupid &^%%ing festival and I felt irrational dislike for many of the people associated with it.

HOW I REPAIRED FOUR YEARS

Twelve months after we left the festival, Phil and I started practising gratitude and, eventually, we began to see a different side to life, a very different one.

We wondered, given we could use gratitude to improve the moment we were in, could we use gratitude to improve the past?

So we gave it a shot. Together we started talking about all the good things that had happened during the four years I directed the film festival. We talked, we laughed, we wrote stuff down. Good memories came flooding back and, some of them surprised us. In our pain we had both forgotten so many wonderful things.

We'd had the privilege of seeing a town come together to create this magical event. We made life-long friends and experienced how supportive a small town can be to strangers. One of the really great things we discovered was how devoted the locals were to volunteering. It was a revelation to us that people who already had full-time jobs were willing to work such long hours as volunteers on this event.

We also had unbelievable support from our family. I doubt that we'd have had anyone attend the first year if Ang hadn't decided to offer her PR services. Our eldest daughter and her husband are gifted professionals in their fields of graphic design and photography and gave generously of their gifts. These three made a huge contribution to the festival - volunteering their time and, when doing paid work, invoicing at a fraction of their standard fees. They set a high professional standard throughout the festival.

Our two youngest daughters, who still lived at home then, cheerfully put up with an absent mother and supported Phil and I in so many ways. Having our children and family involved in this dream was the best of icing on a wonderful cake. They made it extra special.

Even all I shared in chapter one doesn't begin to cover the special things that happened in our lives through our involvement with the festival. As festival director I attended a number of overseas' events and one was pretty spectacular.

One year I flew to Oxford and attended the *Skoll World Forum for Social Entrepreneurs.* This event is attended by some of the world's most amazing people. Jimmy Carter, Al Gore and a number of Nobel Prize winners were also attending the year I did. The founder of TED was there, as was the director of the Sundance Film Festival. These were all people committed to changing the world. The stories I heard there and the people I met were amazing.

I was most dazzled to meet Dr Paul Farmer, a doctor from Haiti who I think might be one of the most inspiring people I've ever come across. I already thought this before I went to Skoll, so imagine how miraculous it felt when I was able to spend the better part of two days in his beautifully humble company. If you want to read about Dr Farmer get yourself a copy of *'Mountains Beyond Mountains'* by Tracey Kidder. That I could have forgotten this experience is kind of unbelievable.

What blew us away was that, comparatively, the bad stuff was a very small part of a brilliant once-in-a-lifetime experience.

In time, as our stories changed, we saw a new perspective and our rage disappeared. We stopped our mad regret and came to value the festival, the town and the people in the same way we had before all the problems.

What I discovered about the sad, angry stories I was telling was they were keeping me imprisoned in the past pain. Every time I told those stories I was hurting myself, to say nothing of what I was doing to the reputation of those I told those stories about.

I had to come to the point where I realised there was no point hanging on to these stories any more and I just stopped telling them. If I do find myself telling one, I'll stop and remind myself this is possibly fiction, definitely biased in my favour and absolutely not worth the pain.

How lovely it's been to have less trolls and villains living in my head. In chapter 16 I'll tell you a little more about how the whole festival fiasco was finally laid to rest.

When I stop the sad, mad stories there are two great extra bonuses; firstly, I have room in my head to start telling myself the stories of the good things I've done, the victories and the conquests. Instead of bemoaning my fate, and telling myself all my victim shit, I get to be the hero for a change, even if only in my head. Sometimes, exactly what I need is to be kinder to myself.

Secondly, I get to contribute in positive ways to the lives of others when I tell the good and life-giving stories about the people I know. Gielan's book points out how much power your words have to change others:

> *'There is a compelling case showing us that we actually change people all the time. And when we fully realize this, we start to see how powerful we are to get others unstuck, see that their behavior matters, and start taking steps to create happiness and success in their lives.'*

SIGNALLING THE STORY

I was reading a great article in *Tech Insider* recently about Brenè Brown's five word hack for relationships. It's brilliant and Brenè says it's her #1 hack:

> *'If I could give men and women in relationship and leaders and parents one hack, I would give them, "the story I'm making up." Basically, you're telling the other person your reading of the situation – and simultaneously admitting that you know it can't be 100% accurate. It's a life-saver for a few reasons, it's honest, it's transparent, and it's vulnerable.'*

It's so simple, I love it. What I like is that in '*Rising Strong*' Brenè gives a whole load of great suggestions as to how to use this simple hack - it's a hack with a plan! Check out the book, you'll find it on my book list.

I think back now to how many times I could have saved myself a ridiculous amount of angst and many clashes by just phrasing things this wise way. 'The story I'm making up about the festival is…'. This is something you can even whisper to yourself when you start telling yourself those painful stories about how awful you are . 'The story I'm making up about me is…'. How refreshing. Brenè's idea makes it so much easier to see what we're up to.

Of course, especially when we take a new road, it isn't easy. Ponder Brenè's words when you next face a story-telling test:

> *'If you're thinking this sounds too hard, I get it. The reckoning can feel dangerous because you're confronting yourself – the fear, aggression, shame and blame. Facing our stories takes courage. But owning our stories is the only way we get to write a brave new ending.'*

PRACTICE

Start stories with 'The story I'm making up is...'

Yep, let's get with the plan. Signal a story is happening. Hold loosely to the lot of it. Check out Brenè's book so you can get more wisdom on this, you'll find it on my book list.

You can also yell my little secret mantra if you'd like a backup practice. Both of these practices will help you edge away from blame and excuses.

No more excuses.

No more blame.

And I'm not playing the sad story game.

I let it all go!

Now you can jump up and down and breathe a huge sigh of relief.

Not actually such a secret mantra is it?

'We have no
more right to put our
discordant states of mind into
the lives of those around us and
rob them of their sunshine
and brightness
than we have to enter their
houses and steal their
silverware.'

JULIA MOSS SETON

14

THE BRUTE MAGNET

In this chapter, I'm in very familiar territory, it's a subject I know really, really well. Complaining. Complaining can be a huge relationship wrecker and, while we're at it, happiness wrecker, so I'm devoting a whole chapter to it. If you're thinking you'll skip this one, please don't.

QUEEN OF COMPLAINING

I could have won awards in complaining. I was like the Queen of Complaining and even now I might get a job as Court Jester of Whining if such a job existed and I were to apply.

I perfectly matched Guy Winch's picture of chronic complainers

Optimists see: A glass half full.

Pessimists see: A glass half empty.

Chronic complainers see: A glass that is slightly chipped holding water that isn't cold enough, probably because it's tap water when I asked for bottled water and wait, there's a smudge on the rim, too, which means the glass wasn't cleaned properly and now I'll probably end up with some kind of virus. Why do these things always happen to me?!

Guy Winch is a psychologist, speaker and author of '*The Squeaky Wheel: Complaining the Right Way to Get Results, Improve Your Relationships and Enhance Self-Esteem*'.

It would have been around 22 years ago that I first had some light thrown on my serial complaining. I was reading, *'Wouldn't Take Nothing For My Journey Now'*, by Maya Angelou, and came across this quote:

'Whining is not only graceless, but can be dangerous. It can alert a brute that there is a victim in the neighbourhood.'

Yes, I admit, I have some very strange goals.

Knowing and understanding grace was one of my life goals so this quote captured my attention. I committed it to memory and I pondered it. Then pondered it some more.

I talked to friends about what Maya had said because I knew I didn't really 'get' it, and I was right, that revelation wouldn't happen for another 15 years.

I'd say to my friends, 'I read this quote and I know it has an important message for me, one day I'll get the understanding.' Then I'd tell them the quote.

I'm pretty sure they wanted to fall to the ground laughing because I had somehow failed to understand what was so clearly written.

Of course, I could see the quote was telling me not to complain and I took note of that message. I started listening to myself and was shocked to find that a lot of the time I was 'gracelessly whining' about pretty much anything.

Once I'd realised I had an issue with complaining I decided to stop doing it, for a while at least. Truth is, I quickly returned to complaining primarily because I couldn't think of what I'd have left to talk about if I stopped.

Seriously!

The fact I could find little to talk about other than whining should have horrified me, instead I just went on complaining.

This sort of thing has happened to me many times in my life. There'll be a 'knock at the door' from God, the Universe, The Great Spirit or Whoever, letting me know there's an issue at hand. I'll pay attention for a little while and then it's like the light fades and I can't really recall what the fuss was about.

So even though I ignored the message of the Maya quote, I continued to talk about and ponder it until one night, almost 17 years later, it eventually bore fruit.

I was at a dinner with a group of friends, sitting at one end of a long table with about 15 other people. It was a fine night in many ways. Beautiful people, wonderful food, balmy weather and joyous conversation. We were having fun, fun, fun and then in walked a man who wrecked it all.

He was a big man in all senses of the word. Tall, broad and brainy. A university professor, a man of knowledge, well travelled, and well regarded. He walked in and seated himself at the opposite end of the table to me and immediately launched into a litany of complaint.

For me the room changed suddenly and it was as though I had a brief glimpse into the 'other world' because I could actually see the joy in the room being sucked out like big swirls of smoke.

And when I glanced over at this man I saw, not a man, but a pathetic little whiney victim, he seemed almost a child he was so vulnerable. He was prey.

Maya's quote came immediately to mind and I finally 'got' that when I complain I announce my commitment to victimhood.

I declare it to the world and I invite confirmation of the fact from the brutes around me.

It's a moment I'll never forget and ever after it was the cowardly victim who I saw whenever I spent time with that 'big' man.

I was very affected, also, by how powerful such a few words of complaint were. They literally sucked joy from the room, whoosh, and it was gone. Interestingly, and I guess sadly, after he spoke we didn't return to the conviviality we'd experienced earlier in the evening.

I'd love to report that I stopped complaining immediately and have never whined again, however I'd be lying. I did, and still do, have to work on complaining less. I am no longer interested in being a victim and I am, these days, considerably improved. I'm also someone who has quite a way to go.

BUT COMPLAINING IS FUN!

Yes, I know! It can be, why do you think I've done it so much? It lets off steam, can bond people, serves as an icebreaker, and has the delightful, yet unfortunate, effect of making us feel somewhat superior to whoever we're complaining about.

I treat complaining a bit like a recreational drug, enjoyable now and then though, if indulged in too often, it can easily become addictive. Not to mention destructive to your relationships and can really mess with your head. So I'm talking about limits, not complete abstinence.

HANG ON, ISN'T VENTING IMPORTANT?

Yes of course, you need to get whatever is causing you pain out. You need to know people hear you, have time for you and care about what is happening to you. And you, as a friend, child, parent, co-worker or partner offer the same to others.

Sometimes when you complain all you are asking is, 'Do I matter to you?' It might only be a bid for attention and, within limits, that's fine. However, constantly 'bidding' and wanting to be the centre of everyone's attention while dancing on a stage of negativity isn't the best way to get your needs met.

SOLVING OR AGGRAVATING?

I need to define what I mean by complaining because not everything that's usually referred to as complaint would come under what I'm talking about here.

In my book! Duh! I finally get where this saying comes from. Ha!

This evening I was out at a restaurant and two pear ciders were ordered yet two apple ciders were delivered to the table. I politely told the waiter of the mistake and handed him the apple ciders. By bringing the issue to the attention of the waiter we were able to enjoy what we'd ordered. I'd do the same if it was a steak or any other situation where I'm not getting what I paid for. In my book it's communication not complaint.

However, if the same scenario happened and I'd been rude, yelled at the waiter, whinged to everyone at the table, badmouthed the restaurant, or become angry or abusive to management (or anyone for that matter) then I've strayed well into the realm of what I'm referring to as complaint.

Simply put; negatively charged exchanges about problems probably fall into the complaint bucket, whereas reasonable communication of facts about the same issue probably wouldn't.

I'm sure there are always examples in either option that break the rule so let's not get picky.

Here is the big difference: communication seeks to solve the issue while complaint aggravates it.

Taking action on things that need taking action on doesn't constitute complaint. Speaking up about injustice, righting wrongs, being socially or politically active doesn't equal complaint.

Whereas whinging about the government without any positive action, endlessly bemoaning the unfairness of life, dooming and glooming social occasions with your take on world politics could well be under the 'graceless whining' banner.

I'm the last person who would encourage you to lie down and take it, to not speak up when you should. If you have problems take action, action isn't moaning to friends and co-workers though. Action is speaking to someone who can do something about it. The boss for instance, or your partner, or the shop that didn't deliver.

Or the guy with our pear ciders.

Moaning to your friends about your partner's failings, or your other friends' failings won't change anything for good. It'll probably make you all a little bit unhappier though.

RATHER LIKE BAD BREATH

Unloading when tough stuff happens isn't necessarily complaint. Unloading about the same thing again and again or to multiple people might come into the complaint category.

After I left the Film Festival, for the next twelve months, pretty much all I wanted to do was talk about the injustice of what had happened. I was desperate for people to see my side, take my side, back me up and reassure me I wasn't at fault.

I went from unloading, which was comforting, necessary and understandable, to obsession. I went over and over and over the same things with the same people and probably bored them to death. I'd even regale new acquaintances with this sad story. I took my victim role very seriously. For a whole year.

People really don't want to hear your problems repeatedly and it's just plain selfish and narcissistic to expect everyone to patiently listen while you moan and groan about your unique tragedies again and again.

I laughed so hard when I found this quote by Lou Holtz.

> *'Don't tell your problems to people, eighty percent don't care and the other twenty percent are glad you have them.'*

It's easy to get into thoughtless habits around complaining.

A common one is coming home from work and telling your partner, yet again, about the downside of your boss, your co-workers and your day in general. You feel great, you've unloaded, hooray!

Yet your partner is stuck with all your negatives on top of their own struggles. To make it worse, the situation doesn't really change much from day-to-day and you're essentially repeating what you said yesterday, and the day before.

It is these seemingly insignificant thoughtless habits that, in the end, often destroy first the fun, then, over many years, the relationship.

Complaining is rather like bad breath. You're not all that aware of it, though others around you are reeling when you open your mouth.

THE INVITATION TO POVERTY

Doris Day is credited with saying 'Gratitude is riches and complaint is poverty'. I am in utter agreement with her.

When I complain I've automatically cancelled any enjoyment, beauty, gratitude, fun and wonder from being experienced in that situation and I've plunged myself into a form of poverty. I've also made sure a few other people have been suddenly poverty stricken, even if only temporarily.

Phil and one of our sons both had jobs at the same place for a few years. They loved having this opportunity to work together and travelled to and from work in the same car. Their boss was a particularly onerous man and eventually their struggles with him became their main topic of conversation. They began a duet of complaining that went on for a very long time.

Every day after work there were new complaints – though on analysis the complaints were really the same ones rehashed in new versions. The complaining drained the life out of us all.

I dithered between wanting to wring their necks (nicely of course) and complaining along with them.

This is serious stuff when you think about it.

You've only got a few brief moments on this earth and if I complain to you I've just sucked the joy out of that moment for you. These are moments you'll never get back.

You only have a limited number of moments to dance or hold hands or wake up or cook dinner with the ones you love. You only have a limited number of times you'll ever go skiing, or bike riding, or to the pub with your friends, or eat croissants, or visit your favourite beach or snuggle in bed, or play hide and seek with your child, or visit your mother. You only have a limited number of trips in the car with your dad.

Or, as with Phil and our son, there were only a few precious days working in the same workplace. Looking back I'm sure they both regret squandering some of the rich and wonderful times they had working together.

Complaining makes it difficult for you, and those around you, to experience 'the good life'.

A DESTRUCTIVE FORCE

Maya Angelou had a deep understanding about the power of words and this made her especially wise in the area of complaining.

Dr Angelou believed words had ongoing effect and lodged inside us, sometimes doing damage. If someone made derogatory jokes, complained or criticised others while visiting her home she'd either invite them to leave or stop them mid-sentence and say, 'Not in my house, you won't.'

Maya didn't want those words cluttering up her life.

She well knew that complaining is a destructive force, and you know it too. If you've ever worked in an office you know the negative power of a few disgruntled workers who join forces. Cliques are formed that can cruelly shun others. People are judged, rejected, dissected and gossiped about. Reputations are ruined. Some people never recover from the pain inflicted when others complain and gossip, often unfairly, about them. Workwise, productivity goes down, morale goes down and profits go down. The business suffers.

Often all this occurs simply because no one bothered to take a problem to the appropriate person who could solve it.

THE UNDERMINING OF TRUST

I often ask people who are complaining to me about a mutual friend or acquaintance why they don't go to the person and talk about the problem directly. Their usual response is 'Oh, I don't want to risk the relationship', or 'I don't want to upset or hurt him/her'. And I assume by those comments that the friendship is one they want to keep intact. There are two things that can make whining to friends about friends a very bad idea.

Firstly, breaking trust by going behind a friend's back is unlikely to contribute to a flourishing friendship. Knowing you've been talked about is upsetting and hurtful in a way that's likely more damaging than going directly to someone and sharing your heartfelt concerns.

Secondly the relationship is naturally distanced and put at risk by problems being unaddressed. Sure, you go off and talk to someone else, you feel a little better and you go back to the friendship. Over time the problem rears its head again and again, you complain to others about it and continue with the friendship. However the problem keeps affecting the friendship. And eventually a big distance grows between you because of the unaddressed issue.

Either way you risk the relationship.

One option is respectful, inclusive and honest. The other is not.

I've made this mistake many times and paid for it dearly in the sort of ways I've mentioned here. I know! Not ideal.

While I've always been an advocate of going to the source and dealing directly with the problems, I've recently allowed some less-than-ideal outcomes to affect me and have resorted to complaint and gossip instead.

COMPLAIN TO BLAME

One of the best arguments against complaint is that when you complain you're more likely to blame.

And blame is a seductive and toxic habit that will limit your career options, destroy relationships, hurt other people, and, perhaps most importantly, stunt your growth as a human being.

YOU'LL BE LESS ATTRACTIVE

I'll get back to the answer in a sec.

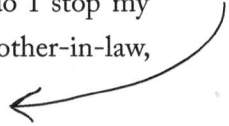

I've been running workshops for over six years and the only question I've had come up repeatedly is, 'How do I stop my _________ (insert co-worker, partner, child, mother-in-law, friend, boss) complaining to me?'

It appears that people, or at least the sort who attend my workshops, hate hearing complaints. By and large people don't rush to seek the company of complainers, in fact whining can make you very unattractive to others.

Well, except for brutes that is, you'll always be able to attract a brute if you're complaining.

REWIRED FOR NEGATIVITY

As I've already mentioned, your brain is plastic, changeable and devoted to taking the easy, most used, neural pathways.

When you complain you build pathways with negatives and your brain will, in time, default to those negative pathways if you use them often enough. When you have pathways wired around negativity those pathways cause your brain to scan for negatives and you'll find them.

You'll become better and better at finding problems. And those problems won't only be with your workplace, the make of your car, the size of your thighs and insanity of politicians. They'll also be with all the people in your life.

You'll be quicker to pick up on their faults, their failings and the ways they let you down which is a great way to become unhappy in a relationship.

Cut down your complaining and you'll open up the possibility of improving all your relationships.

THAT QUESTION

You may also have the same question that so many people coming to my workshops have, 'How do I stop my ______ complaining all the time?'

There are plenty of things you can do and I'll share the two I find most effective with chronic complainers.

Listen and Ask

The worst thing you can do to a chronic complainer (or anyone for that matter) is to dismiss or belittle them. Listen, nod, show you care, because, as I said earlier, this might be all they are after. When you tell the person complaining that 'It's nothing to worry about?' or you've told them they're foolish or wrong. That isn't what anyone wants to hear. They may even ramp up their complaints to try to get you to understand how dire their unique situation is.

So provided I haven't belittled them or fallen into the tempting trap of joining in the whiney party and adding my own negative insights, then I've earned the right to ask the question:

> *'So what are you going to do about it?'*

And I keep going back to that question.

The complainer has two choices. They can keep complaining to me and I'll listen with interest and come back to the same, by then annoying, question or they can stop complaining to me.

Maybe they'll even wake up to the fact that they aren't a victim. Maybe they'll understand they have a choice and there is plenty they can do to change the situation.

You never know. Either way I won't have to listen for long.

Divert

Depending on the nature of the relationship I might take a different tack. With close friends I feel free to say, 'Ok, enough complaining, let's talk about something else now.' They're pretty familiar with my journey and are just relieved I don't complain as much as I used to, so this works out fine.

With others I'm more likely to attempt to, at an opportune moment, deflect the conversation to another topic or even change the topic by asking them a question related to something else. Sometimes I even ask them to tell me about the good stuff in their life.

To be honest, this asking about the good stuff has mixed results.

THE PRACTICE

The One a Day Whinge

Cut your complaining down to one whinge a day. Make it a good one. Before you whinge you'll have to decide if this whinge is worth wasting your one whinge on. That makes it fun, especially in a workplace where everyone is doing the same thing.

I've had reports that the corridors ring with the question 'Is this your one-a-day-whinge? Do you think it's really worth wasting your whinge on that?'

'There isn't
time, so brief is life,
for bickerings, apologies,
heartburnings, callings to account.
There is only time for loving,
and but an instant,
so to speak,
for that.'

MARK TWAIN

15

THE BEST ADVICE

Did you know that every second your brain is exposed to 11 million bits of information but it can only process about 40 bits a second? There is a lot happening out there you don't know about. What this means is that your brain has to choose which bit to process and attend to and which huge amount to dismiss and ignore. I learned this from another of my favourite authors, and a man I mentioned in an earlier chapter, Shawn Achor. He's an exceptional speaker and has a brilliant, funny TED talk you might enjoy.

Mentioning Shawn reminds me of something I wanted to say about authors, teachers and speakers, so I'm going to divert here for a minute. It's easy, when we read a fabulous book or hear an incredible speaker, to think they're some sort of guru or special people who are elevated above the likes of ordinary people. Better, more 'together' people than you are. Guess what? They're not. I know this is true because of two things. Firstly, the obvious one, I'm a speaker and this book makes me a writer. Secondly, I've met many of these famous people while speaking at conferences and conducting interviews.

Here's what I've learned; those of us who write and speak and teach are writing, speaking and teaching in the areas of our greatest failings. We are writing, speaking and teaching the lessons that we learn, and are still learning and often need to re-learn on a daily basis. None of the teachers, speakers and authors I've met are any more special than you. They still fail in the areas they are authorities on. Isn't this wonderful? It gave me so much hope to learn this.

True, some of the writers, speakers and teachers I've met do seem to have forgotten their frailties and fallen for the hype on their book covers.

Yeah, when I'm not reading I'm sitting around dropping names.

Most, I'm happy to report, remain well connected to the earth and are delightful humans, aware they're on the very same journey as the rest of humanity. Shawn Achor is one such delightful human. He's also very generous. He actually allowed Phil and I to impinge on one of his most private and precious times. He was in Australia with his very new wife, author Michelle Gielan whose wonderful book I mentioned in chapter 14, and we actually gatecrashed their honeymoon. Not that sort of gatecrash! We just all had dinner together, which was very special. I mean what sort of kindness is it to be that inclusive?

THE BEST ADVICE

Okay, back to the topic. I'm telling you about these 'bits' just in case you've forgotten blind spots from chapter four, because I wanted you to be open to what I'm going to suggest. I thought if you realised how little info you are really getting on a day-to-day, or second-to-second basis, you'd see the wisdom in taking advice. Maybe you'll even intentionally seek advice!

When a friend or family member gives you their honest opinion on your situation, especially if it wasn't asked for, and especially if they top their opinion with a little advice, you might be tempted to be affronted, offended and reject what they've told you.

You might feel as if they've interfered where they have no right to interfere. You might be angered by their arrogance in thinking they have something you need to hear. You might just think they're too stupid to know anything about your situation. You might have thoughts that would lead you to take no notice of their suggestion. That's understandable. You might even be right. Maybe they are arrogant, or stupid or interfering, however you'll only stick to that stance if you've forgotten about blind spots or didn't understand my opening paragraph. Here, I'll spell it out:

You're missing most of the information.

Anyone who comes along and can give you another angle, another view, or a bit more information is an angel. Entertain them! It doesn't really matter if you like them, trust them, love them or admire them. Listen anyway, sometimes our enemies are our enemies for good reason and they may know something you don't.

You don't have to take any notice of what they say or do what they suggest, however, listening and considering won't cost you anything and may pay big dividends.

SHUT UP DONNA!

Imagine this. My friend Donna comes to me with a bit of advice, 'Hey, you're not much of a catch', and I get offended and go sulk. Later I complain to everyone about what a rude, insensitive, know-it-all bitch she is and I never speak to her again.

I win.

Well, you know I don't win. I lose. I lose big time. I lose the chance to act on the best advice I'd ever get. I lose Mr Wonderful, I lose our precious children. I lose my life simply because I'm too proud to listen and take the blow.

ADVICE FROM MY MUM

In February this year I was having coffee with my darling mother. She lives around the corner and is an unfailing source of excellent advice. I treasure having her in my life, partly because of her wise guidance.

Her delivery, however, could do with some polishing.

Over coffee she said, 'Toni, you look like Ten Tonne Tessie, you look awful. You need to dress for your figure and stop wearing those baggy clothes.' Okay, so there's some truth in what she says. I was embarrassed about recent weight gain and I had been trying to cover it up.

Still that was pretty harsh advice and I was a little dumbfounded. I wasn't sure if I should laugh or cry. A few minutes later I had to laugh because she complimented the waitress then turned to me and said, 'I've decided to compliment everyone I meet today.' I replied with 'Mum! So what was that you said to me? A compliment?' She rolled her lovely eyes at me and said, 'No darling, that was the truth.'

A few days later I went shopping and bought shorter dresses and more fitted clothes. Ever since then people keep telling me how much weight I've lost. I laugh to myself, and silently thank my mum, because only I know I've actually put on five kilos since February.

I'm definitely going to stop eating pork crackling shortly, I am, really I am.

AN ALLIANCE OF ADVISERS

If you are really smart and not too much of a cry-baby then encircling yourself with an alliance of advisers is one way to really change your life. They will see the things you either cannot or will not see. They can be your best blessing.

Or not. They might give you shit advice too, that's okay. Listen, take it to heart, think about it, weigh it up and you decide. You're deep down wise, and the right arrow will hit the mark, you'll know. Besides if you have an alliance you can check out the advice with another person.

On top of an alliance I pretty much listen to anyone's advice, you never know quite when an angel has been sent with exactly the right thing for you. Of course I then dismiss a lot of that input too – not everyone is an angel!

As I said in an earlier chapter, I've had some excellent advice over the years. I now know how to eat mangoes without the mess and how to get red wine stains out of white carpet. However, given the nature of this book I've restricted myself to a few of the most helpful pieces of advice I've had regarding relationships.

You'll find this advice spread over the next two chapters. I've had so much great advice it's been tough trying to work out what to include.

ADVICE FROM A MENTOR

Expectations are resentments in the making

One of the very delightful things to come out of the festival was our ongoing relationship with actor Tony Barry. In the first year we'd been looking for a festival patron and one of our regular jurors, the wonderful Aussie icon, Caroline Jones, suggested Tony. He was the perfect patron. He understood the vision of the festival in a way very few people did.

Tony is a unique individual with a talent for oration that is incredible. His passion for society's weaker ones is remarkable and I know he's invested every aspect of his life into the lives of others and rarely taken time or money to pamper himself.

I've met many people and there aren't many I admire in the way I admire this man.

He is wise. Truly wise. He came into my life not long after my gorgeous father died, so he's become a mix of father and friend and one, thankfully, not backward with speaking his interesting mind. We saw him at the festival each year and during the year we'd get together in beautiful Byron Bay.

He was, I think, the only person who could see where things were headed. Tony warned me a few times over the years, 'Toni, this will end in tears, they'll get rid of you.' This was incomprehensible to me. Who in their right mind gets rid of the visionary?

Umm, well, let me think... Apple?

Who in their right mind gets rid of the person donating an additional 40 to 60 hours of work a week on top of their paid hours? Who in their right mind gets rid of the one person who has given their whole heart to the project?

No one, right? I couldn't see that happening anytime soon. I ignored his lone voice.

Writing the word 'visionary' reminded me of something hilarious one of our most devoted volunteers related to me after I left the festival. Very worried about the future of the festival he asked one of the board members, 'What are we going to do about a visionary now?' She replied, 'Oh we're going to get one of the volunteers to do that job.'

Tony was a source of strength, support and wisdom after all the shit hit the fan. He was the one who told me it was a gift in shitty wrapping paper. He knew. He was a man well acquainted with suffering and he'd allowed it to make him compassionate, gentle and a tireless fighter for good.

People become truly rich when they allow suffering to be their friend.

People often tell me I'm outspoken, and I am, though compared to Tony Barry I'm a quiet little bird. This man is the Voice! He tells you exactly what's on his mind and exactly what he observes.

One day I was whining away to him, afloat in my sea of self-pity and hanging on tight to my victim raft. He'd had enough of my self-indulgence and looked me in the eye and said, 'Toni, expectations are resentments in the making,' and he said it like a slap in the face.

Yay, I had another bit of wisdom to ponder, and ponder I did. I started looking through my list of resentments and found, to my amazement, yes actual amazement, that every one of them was connected to an expectation! Over half my life was gone and I'd never made this connection before. What a gift Tony Barry, thank you.

This was like lifting up a nice large round rock you like to sit on and finding out it was the home of a lot of nasty, biting, vicious spiders and snakes. I'd been sitting there without a clue of the danger nearby.

I was sitting on so many petty resentments, and that was without even beginning to include the ones to do with the festival.

It's easy stuff to get lost in. Women expect husbands to admire their new dress. Men might expect her to be ready for sex without notice. And have you ever expected people to like you and felt resentment when they didn't? What about your parents, have you had expectations of them they didn't deliver on?

When I started thinking about it, my expectation list was ridiculous – a whole stack of things I thought were just normal.

'I expected them to be grateful.'

'I expected them to listen.'

'I expected them to care.'

'I expected her to notice me.'

'I expected them to be on time.'

This was just last week, not mentioning any names though.

'I expected him to remember to pick me up from the airport.'

This was happening everywhere – I expected the house to be clean, my friends to call me, the dishwasher to have been stacked the way I preferred. I expected cards, presents, calls, attention, to be top priority and have instant service from my phone provider.

I expected to be loved in return when I loved, I expected my friends to have my back at all times, I expected people to be honest with me and I expected people to explain themselves to me.

When we expect people to be a lot more perfect than they are how can the outcome be anything but disappointment and resentment?

Who was I to think all these people needed to continually bow down to my expectations? A lot of things I thought were normal I now question. I could see how in my quest to have my expectations met, I was bullying people. Mostly it was subtle bullying such as, 'I need you to tell me what's going on, you have to tell me,' yet it was bullying none the less.

Not that I've got expectations under control by a long shot. I am more conscious of this tendency and, whenever I notice the resentment, I track it back to the source and let go of the expectation. This is an ongoing practice I imagine will be lifelong. I now see more clearly the connection between my struggle to be grateful and expectation.

If I let go of expectation then every good thing someone does is a gift that I appreciate in a way I don't when an expectation is met.

THEY HURT ME AGAIN!

I really love, love, love this quote by Maya Angelou:

'When someone shows you who they are believe them; the first time.'

If you're not familiar with this quote, ponder it for a while. It contains a great truth that we often fail to get. Are you angry at someone's unkindness to you, yet you've experienced their unkindness before? If so, don't blame them. If you already know who they are and still choose to hang out with them then they're not the problem. You can't keep expecting them to be suddenly different.

If you want to play in the sandpit with them and they take your spade, don't start crying. You knew and you chose. It's madness to keep getting disappointed when they behave exactly as they've already told you they'd behave.

GREAT EXPECTATIONS

Of course there are expectations you can and will have. Need to have. Your boss has expectations that you turn up to work and you have expectations that you will be paid.

Society couldn't work without expectations being met.

This sort of expectation is clearly communicated, your role is defined and remuneration, time off and certain perks are agreed upon. If your boss defaults on what is expected of him you'll take some action and your boss shouldn't be surprised. Your wage is expected in your account and there'll be other people getting involved if it doesn't turn up.

It's all the additional expectations your boss isn't aware of that are more likely to cause strife and resentment. While it was never agreed on, you probably expected your boss to be kind to you. You expected praise for your effort on each project. You expected promotion within a few years.

When these expectations, that were not communicated let alone agreed on, are assumed, you create fertile ground for resentment.

You're vulnerable enough to unrealistic expectations at work but when you get home expectations can come from many unconscious layers. Add gender stereotypes, ideals about family, what you think makes a good parent or partner and all the other patterns pulling you around, then you can have crops of expectation coming up everywhere.

We don't even know we think certain things.

1950s HOUSEWIFE

For the past 20 years Phil has done most of the cooking. For the first 20 years he did virtually none. He took up cooking because he had to, there were five kids and I was ill for a few years, so someone had to do it. Unexpectedly, he discovered he loved cooking and so I, who happen to dislike cooking, handed the job over with relief. I would much rather do dishes and clean up than cook.

In the past 20 years I could not even count the hundreds of people who've told me how lucky I am that Phil cooks for me. It is a constant comment. Of course, I wholeheartedly agree, I *am* lucky he cooks for me. However, and this is where the sneaky gender bias rears its ugly head, I don't think anyone has ever said to him how lucky he is I clean up afterward. And I'm pretty sure that no one, in the first 20 years when I cooked thousands of tasty meals, ever said to Phil or my kids, 'You are so lucky to have your mum/wife cook for you.'

I've told the broadest range of people that Phil cooks for me and I get the same response every time, 'You're so lucky! What luxury.' Yet I'd be willing to bet that most of those people don't feel they have 1950s' attitudes to a woman's role in the home. I'll take it further; I'm willing to bet most of those people are sure they don't have 1950s' attitudes to women.

So many of our expectations are unconscious, that's why you'll need to track back and find out what is behind your resentments.

ADVICE FROM MY BUSINESS MENTOR

Don't give unasked for advice

My advice, in this chapter, to get lots of advice is not, and I repeat, not, advice to give advice.

It's like this – most people don't like someone giving them advice, especially if it wasn't asked for. It can send the message that you don't have faith in their abilities or wisdom. I had to learn this one the hard way.

As I said earlier in the book, I've done this a lot. A lot! It was my business mentor who explained to me that advice can feel like a judgment to the people you're advising. This has been such a hard one for me to really 'get' because I love advice so much that I truly think I'm being kind. In fact even some offers of help can be interpreted as judgement. No wonder people didn't respond so well to my 'helpfulness'.

So pretty much use this as a rule of thumb; unless they've recently read this book, hold off on the unasked for advice. Also, I feel it's advisable (ha ha) to warn you even if it's asked for advice, they may not like it. In fact, even if they read this book they may not like your advice.

Make deposits, let people know they're valued instead. Unless you've been invited into an alliance of advisors that is.

I've just realised I'm writing a book that gives advice! I've got it bad!

PRACTICE

Spring Clean Your Resentments

I was Googling 'resentment' while writing this chapter, as one does, and found that one of the 12 steps in AA is to list your resentments then see your role in the outcome. You can Google 'Resentment List' and find one ready to print. I'd add the extra column to link it specifically to an expectation if I were you. Though I'm not you, so give it a miss if you like. I'm sure this practice will key right into the advice on forgiveness.

You'll feel amazing when you've done this. Send me an email and let me know how it went.

'Laughter is
more than just
a pleasurable activity...
When people laugh together,
they tend to talk and touch more
and to make eye contact
more frequently.'

GRETCHEN RUBIN

THE HAPPINESS PROJECT

16

WHAT A FEELING!

In this chapter I want to have a look at a few of the keys to sanity in relationships. I'm giving you a brief touch on huge subjects that could well each be a book on their own.

ACCEPTANCE

So many people have spoken to me about my need to accept various situations. That's because it is the hardest of lessons for me to embrace. I'm the 'change the world' type and people like me are driven to change the status quo. We see the wrongs and we want to right them. We see the faults and we want to fix them. We see the problems and we want to solve them. We barely sit down, let alone contemplate, because we're too busy taking action.

Acceptance can feel as though I'm going against my very nature. Yet, if I want some inner peace, good relationships and freedom from resentment then acceptance is exactly what I need to embrace.

I was watching an interview with an elderly couple on Youtube the other day. They were being interviewed on their 81st wedding anniversary. The woman commented, 'Marriage isn't a lovey-dovey thing you know. You've learned to accept one another's ways of life. Agreements and disagreements, you accept. These days people expect miracles of each other.

You know, like, "You have to agree with me, this is what I want". But it doesn't work that way. We're all different.'

Acceptance is key to flourishing relationships. Acceptance bridges our differences and allows love to cross over.

THE INVISIBLE LASSO

Remember Graeme Long, pastor at Sydney's famous Wayside Chapel, who I mentioned in chapter five in relation to the prisoners? The same interview ranged across many subjects and one was acceptance. Long talked about how crucial acceptance was to allow the process of change to happen in others. I thought what he said was very profound.

'Once people see that there are others with them, and for them, people change on their own.'

The usual foolhardy thing we do as humans, when we encounter things we don't like in ourselves or in others, is to resist the thing we don't like. We try to fix it, change it, annihilate it, help it, hide it, erase it, remove it and/or tackle it into submission. Unfortunately that doesn't work too well.

When you approach others in this way they'll feel judged and put up walls. When you approach yourself this way you'll feel unworthy and put up walls. Either way there is no love getting in. Either way there is cover up and hiding going on. You'll be hiding your failings and they'll be hiding from your judgement.

Acceptance is, absolutely counter-intuitively, a major key to change.

Forget nagging. Forget pushing others to change. You'll only be compounding the problem. Have you ever noticed when someone has a judgement about you, you behave in exactly that way? I have and it intrigues me. When I'm with people who have contempt for me I say and do incredibly stupid things. When I'm with someone who accepts me, I say and do wiser and more loving things. When I'm in front of a crowd who thinks I'm wonderful, I say and do inspiring things and, interestingly, the opposite is true. I can be an incoherent, forgetful klutz on stage if I feel the audience has a negative judgement about me. I'm sure any actor, speaker, singer and comedian would tell you the same thing.

I have a little pet theory one day scientists will discover that judgement has the power to lock people into certain behaviours. Something like an invisible lasso that flies through the air and wraps around the person, tying them up and forming some sort of prison. I also believe when we cease to judge someone then we set them free. I have nothing to base this on, just my gut.

WHAT A FEELING!

Do you know of a better feeling than being safe in the company of friends who love you? People who know every bit of you and love you anyway? Better still, they accept you? When I'm with our friends, Mark and Karen, I feel amazing because they know all of me and accept me, with open arms and joy, just as I am. What a feeling! I can relax inside.

Do you remember I said in chapter five this sort of love, that is wholeheartedly given despite our faults, is akin to the best of miracles?

Forget akin. Being loved for who we are *is* the best of miracles.

And now I want to throw something a little wild into the ring. Another horseman!

ANOTHER HORSEMAN?

In the original biblical story there were only Four Horsemen of The Apocalypse, which fitted nicely with Dr Gottman's four behaviours. However, I think there is a Fifth Horseman. He used to ride into our house a lot and now, since he's been mostly absent, the level of enmity in our conflicts has dropped considerably.

Before I get to my new Horseman I'll tell you the story of how we discovered the way to close the door on that particular rider.

FIRST SOME HISTORY

Once upon a time people in the world didn't have navigation systems on their phones and had to use things called maps. Maps were large, cumbersome things that, once opened, never again folded up to the original size. Trying to fold a map could cause a meltdown in even the most patient of people. Maps were also very awkward to read while driving.

It was very important, therefore, that each person on earth memorised the way to everywhere because absolutely no one ever wanted to open a map. You don't believe this is possible do you? I know, but remember these were the days of longer attention spans and better memories. Truly, I kid you not. Everyone knew, by heart, the phone numbers and addresses of people in their own families. Some people could even recall their friends' numbers as well. It's true.

And everyone knew the way to everywhere. The trouble was that everyone knew a different way to everywhere and everyone insisted that their way was the best and, of course, the fastest way.

Tragically, for many couples, their marriages disintegrated after being worn down by arguments about which was the shortest way.

THE SHORTEST WAY

Of course, I always knew the shortest way. Always.

One day, many years ago, eons before navigation systems, Phil and I were driving in suburban Sydney. We were late for an important meeting and both became quite stressed. He was in the driver's seat and I was backseat driving. 'Turn left, turn left', I instructed. He drove straight ahead because, for some reason, he was convinced he always knew the shortest way. Always.

An argument ensued that got more heated the later and more lost we became. Eventually even Phil's laid-back nature disappeared and he turned and yelled at me, in a voice I didn't get to hear too often, 'You're so bossy!'

Bossy? Me?

Initially I was incensed. How dare he accuse me of being bossy? I was about to yell back when I had a sudden thought. 'What is the point of continually defending my stance that I'm not bossy?' The truth is that I'm bossy. Very bossy. I also realised that this little skirmish was about to become a battle. Someone was going to get hurt.

In that moment, I could see I had an alternative, one that would leave no wounds. So instead of yelling at him I started to laugh.

'You're right, you're right! I'm so, so, so bossy, I'm the bossiest!' He looked a bit shocked for a second. I wasn't really known for my ability to laugh in the middle of an argument.

Then I said, quite affectionately, 'And you're so stubborn!' He started to laugh too. We forgot about which way was the shortest way and laughed at our silly human selves the remainder of the trip.

LAUGHTER IS THE BEST MEDICINE

The next time a disagreement came up it was Phil who smiled and said sweetly, 'Bossy…' when things started to get heated. I answered with 'Stubborn…' and we started to laugh. Laughter has been the water on the fire for us. Most of our disagreements since that car trip have been laced with laughter. We're frequently in tears of laughter over how bossy or stubborn either of us was being on that particular day. This anonymous quote says it all:

We've been talking about starting a business called 'Bossy & Stubborn' for years.

> *'Every time you are able to find some humour in a situation, you win.'*

Laughter has made us affectionate about each other's faults and much more accepting of our own. I rarely take offence when Phil helps me see I'm behaving like a Muggle because laughter takes away my defensiveness. We've always tried to be kind and respectful during arguments. However it has been laughter, and the affection that laughter fosters, that has made the biggest difference to us.

THE FIFTH HORSEMAN

So, I'm announcing a Fifth Horseman called *Taking Yourself Too Seriously.*

Muggles Take Themselves Too Seriously: If you don't think you have many faults, or you're afraid that admitting your faults will put you at a disadvantage, you might be in Muggle territory.

You'll probably be under the illusion that life is a game you need to win. You'll get confused and think relationships are some sort of competition where being right is actually important. Unfortunately, you won't think it's funny to be wrong and you'll take the whole thing way too seriously. So seriously you'll forget to have fun.

> **Magicians Laugh At Themselves:** As a Magician you know that enjoyment, affection, and love are what life is all about. You look at the big picture, are big hearted, and big on letting things go. You're not laughing at them, just at situations our shared human frailties create. And you're fully aware you are a fragile human and as prone to failure as the next person, and you can laugh about it. You like to lighten the darkness and make people feel safe.

Magicians understand having someone love you is a miracle and they know miracles don't happen every day.

If I notice I've allowed Taking Yourself Too Seriously into the room, I start with some laughter and get over myself. This is not too difficult when I'm with Phil, our trust level is deep, deep, deep. While we do hurt each other now and then, both of us know malice is not at the heart of the action. With others it can be harder to be lighthearted when there is conflict.

It's a funny algorithm. Laughter builds trust and trust allows laughter.

Many of our conflicts either fizzle out or are resolved with generosity if we can get into the laughter zone.

THE ADVICE OF A FRIEND

Forgive, even if an apology never comes.

It's beginning to sound as though I like getting my face slapped isn't it? In one way I do. There is nothing more valuable to me in a friendship than my friend's willingness to say the hard stuff to me. Sure I do get hurt, I feel ashamed and embarrassed and yet I also feel loved. Apparently I am quite unusual in liking to have this sort of input though I'm not fond of people 'should-ing' on me.

Because I had worked through a lot of the emotional baggage around the festival I felt as if I'd really grown a lot. I'd walked through some heavy stuff and come out the other side, somewhat battered for sure, though also a bit wiser. When, two years after the festival, as I mentioned in the first two chapters, some very treasured relationships broke down, I thought I'd be okay, after all I'd matured a bit and learned some new skills hadn't I?

This was true and it also wasn't as true as I'd have liked.

While I didn't let this relationship breakdown take over my life to the extent I had let the festival ending engulf me, it was seriously heavy going for five years. I had to constantly relearn lessons I thought I'd learned, sometimes daily.

I cannot see the word engulf without laughing because I listened to the audio book by David Sedaris called 'Engulfed in Flames'. Very funny.

When we try to sort stuff out with people it doesn't always go well. And then we're stuck. What to do? All this emotion and nowhere to go with it. No resolution on the horizon and no help for the pain.

This pain was so fierce I thought it would kill me. One night, a few years in, I woke up thinking I was having a heart attack and my only thought was, 'Thank God, I'll be free of this pain.' I didn't wake Phil or consider getting medical help. There was no panic or fear; only relief that freedom was coming.

One day a brilliant, brave and honest friend took my face in her hands and told me I had to forgive even if an apology never comes.

Ahh… of course. What was I waiting for?

What did I already know? Blind spots, self-justification, naive realism, bias and just plain forgetting. Self-deception was at work in both me and, quite possibly, with the others involved.

They'd likely never see they owed me an apology and, really, did they even owe me one at all? Maybe it is me who owes them the apology.

Though, in this instance, it was hard to know. I tried the route of attempting to talk it through and that hadn't gone well. Too much pain on both sides I suspect.

Who was I to make them march to my tune regarding apologising or even talking? In my mind their actions were hardhearted and unkind. However when I stopped and thought about it I could see I was back at expectation. I was deciding what was acceptable in this relationship (and really some things *are* unacceptable – if you can't accept them get out of the relationship!) and then judging them by my expectation. I was judging them by my own fabulous ability to see things as they really are – the right way.

I had to at least entertain the idea that their ability to see things as they really are was every bit as valid as my ability to see things as they really are.

The nasty side-effects of expectations are resentment, bitterness and lack of forgiveness. And these were not things I wanted to live with. I needed to relinquish my 'rightness', accept that I didn't know their motives and they might not be the more evil side of the equation. My assessment of the situation might be the wrong one. I might be, like Very Nice, the one who had pushed the button on the explosion. The truth for me is not the truth for them. And neither side will ever know the whole truth. Whatever the truth I needed to forgive even if they never see a reason to apologise.

I doubt the pain will ever entirely go away, and that's ok, pain is a great friend in many ways. It keeps me compassionate, I have more empathy – I need to have pain there.

Forgiving allows you a way back to joy.

There's the additional bonus for all my other relationships as well. I don't have to have that poison inside me that inevitably leaks out on to others.

The same is true with the festival, the pain is there, way less but still there – the loss is felt though the anger is gone. I'm not so addicted to judging the people involved.

I like the way my friend Mark describes forgiveness: 'Forgiveness is when you've dropped the charges'

Forgiveness doesn't mean nothing happened and, in my experience at least, doesn't always remove all the pain.

Remember, forgiving doesn't mean you put yourself in harm's way and it may not restore the relationship. Neither is your forgiveness something you announce to the person you've forgiven because to do that would be a pretty aggressive thing to do and definitely won't help restore the relationship.

I like what TD Jakes said:

'I think the first step is to understand that forgiveness does not exonerate the perpetrator. Forgiveness liberates the victim. It's a gift you give yourself.'

THERE'S A TEACHER IN THE ROOM

The practice of gratitude, which I began after the festival, did give me some new neural pathway options and this has been incredibly useful when I experience a relationship mess.

Now my first thought is much more likely to be; 'Wow, I'm about to learn something amazing', and I know that even being able to see a tough situation in this light is the effect of gratitude.

I find it pays to look around and see if the teacher has entered the room.

Previously when there was unfairness or difficulty in a relationship, I've just felt hard done by. Even noticing there is a teacher is a huge improvement for me.

Now this is a teacher I'm not all that fond of, one that takes me places I'd rather not go. I'm not the outdoors type and she drags me up mountains and I fall off the sides because I forget to hold on to the rope. I end up back at the foot of the mountain and have to start again. I get bruised and cold and very, very tired and I long for the teacher to just leave me alone. Just give me a bed and a doona and leave me alone. Leave me alone.

This teacher never listens to my pleas.

If I do take to my bed and ignore her, she'll just invent a new lesson and come back with another peak to climb. In the end, it's best to put on my hiking boots and get on with it.

Yes this teacher is rough, however she's also amazing and she is the best of teachers. If you can get over your resistance to the tough climb then all sorts of vistas open up.

Pain is our most wonderful teacher.

When I say something like, 'Pain is our most wonderful teacher' I know this makes me sound like some sort of self-flagellating monk. I'm not. I do, however, believe that suffering of any kind helps us see clearly, downsizes our blind spots, knocks out some pride and is very good for treating naive realism. You see? We all need some pain now and then – which is just as well because, life, even a happy one, is full of suffering.

Some pain however, isn't that helpful. The pain of being unable to forgive for one. Accept the fact that an apology isn't likely. Remember the prisoners in chapter five if you need some convincing.

Do you want to suffer for longer? Do you want to wait another two or three years to come to the conclusion they're not going to admit to whatever you think they need to? I'm guessing you don't.

I used to find forgiveness a huge issue. I wanted to forgive people and I'd grit my teeth and do it. It seemed to me like a large ball, one larger than me, one I'd have to roll up a hill. I'd get it nicely settled on the hill and, almost before I'd turned around, the ball would roll down the hill.

Sometimes I'd get flattened as it rolled. So, as soon as I was on my feet again, I'd start back up the hill. It was like Groundhog Day. Sometimes it would be like a prescription: Take one daily.

I'd forgive, and forgive and forgive again. I'd move that ball a bit, and maybe it was a shorter haul up the hill the next time. However there'd *always* be a next time.

These days it's different. Forgiveness is not such an uphill trip. My research did yield the very gold I was after. Forgiveness can be almost effortless if I remember:

I don't remember accurately

They don't remember accurately

I'm biased

They're biased

They know they're telling the truth

I know I'm telling the truth

I see things as they really are

They see things as they really are

They have blind spots

I have blind spots

I know why they did it, and it wasn't very nice

They're sure they know they know my motives, and they aren't good ones

Their expectations weren't met

And neither were mine

I've self-justified

And so have they

They don't think they hurt me very much

I feel they deliberately meant to hurt me

I don't think I hurt them, well not much anyway

They feel very hurt by me

Probably much of the angst I feel is manufactured imaginings coming from the motives I've thoughtfully ascribed to other parties.

Forgiving just makes sense. Why would I continue to create pain for myself? Besides, who knows if there is anything really to forgive? It might have been all in my head.

Even when things aren't in my head, where bad stuff actually happened, such as rape and other traumas, forgiveness is still the essential key to wholeness. It still has to be offered without the other party asking for it.

AND BACK TO THE GOOD NEWS STORY

Phil, wise person that he is, suggested that, to assist in my quest to forgive, I might like to put myself in the shoes of the person who has offended me. So guess what ? I did that with the festival and here is what I thought it would be like to be in their shoes.

We were a pair of strangers who'd come into their town and floated a great idea. One that had appeal to locals for entirely different reasons to our very particular vision. Locals and local business had supported the festival because it was a great event for the town. Which is the same reason the volunteers and most of the board members had supported the festival. They put up with us, the strangers, because we had great ideas and were willing to work hard.

As the festival grew the town took more and more ownership of the wonderful event they'd created. This was a great baby they were raising and she was turning out to be lovelier than they'd imagined. People were invested, excited and terribly proud. Then I started talking about bringing outsiders in. Allowing control of the event to go to people who didn't care about their town. People who'd only met their baby once or twice. The board, and other locals, could see these outsiders could possibly want to take their beautiful baby and bring her up elsewhere.

They became afraid they'd lose their festival and everything they'd worked so hard for. Phil and I had been transparent, from day one, that our mission was to achieve the vision of the festival. While we definitely didn't have any plans to move, or ever want to move the festival, everyone knew we were open to considering a move to another town if it was ever necessary.

I'm thinking that, with outsiders on the board, a move suddenly became a real possibility in the minds of the locals. The best bet, to protect their stakeholders, was to get rid of us.

And you know what?

> If I were in their shoes I'd make exactly the same decision. Who wouldn't? It was the only fair and sensible thing to do.

And here we are back at expectations.

How could we expect this town to work for, and make decisions in favour of, a vision they didn't hold? One that may not directly benefit them. It was a ridiculous expectation.

This putting-on-their-shoes stuff is really useful! Try it. You might find it helps.

PRACTICE

Learn To Laugh At Yourself

If you do tend to get a bit huffy and take it all too seriously then it's time to learn to laugh at yourself. Maybe 'step outside' yourself more often and see how your behaviour might look to you, if you were not you. Is there anything you could make light of instead of being so touchy about it?

Of course you'll do this in a loving way won't you? Be kind to yourself while you're owning your shit.

‘Gratitude
is not only
the greatest of virtues,
but the parent of
all the others.’

MARCUS TULLIUS CICERO

17

THE LOVE POTION

You can get excited now because I've left the best till last.

I've touched on gratitude before, and no self-respecting book on relationships would be complete without this great love potion being mentioned. This will be a very quick look at some of the factors gratitude brings into the relationship mix. If you want to practise the craft and be a Magician then you'll need loads of Love Potion.

Gratitude is the sort of magical power that usually exists only in fiction. Use this power often and you have the ultimate love potion.

I mentioned earlier that Phil and I were doing interviews with world leaders in various fields. Conflicting schedules didn't allow for an in-person interview with Dr Gottman however I did get to talk to him on the phone. I wasn't surprised to hear him say:

'Gratitude is one of the most important things you can do to improve relationships.'

Here are just a few of the many reasons why I agree with Dr Gottman about the power of gratitude in relationships.

THE PROTECTIVE FACTOR

Or you with a magic wand.

Gratitude equips you with the weaponry you need to slay self-pity, victim thinking, disappointment, discontent, jealousy, rage, and all those other nasties that gnaw at your relationships. Picture Luke Skywalker with a lightsaber.

When I take the time to practise gratitude regularly I feel as if I'm wearing armour and many of the emotional slings and arrows in life don't penetrate in the way they often do. When I'm not as vulnerable to feeling rejected or hurt, dismissed, ignored, rejected, or belittled then I do relationships a whole lot better.

THE RATIO FACTOR

Remember Dr Gottman from the Magician chapter? The man who can predict divorce with 90% accuracy? He can do this amazing feat just by looking at data taken from three minutes of observing couples arguing. He doesn't even have to hear what the couple are saying or be in the room with them. He just needs to know the nature of the interaction they have during those three minutes.

Over the years Gottman has observed enough marriages to come up with an equation of positive interactions vs negative ones and knows that these predict the outcome of the union.

You, like most people, might think relationships are a 1:1 equation, that balance and fairness are the keys:

I take the garbage out and you do the laundry

I say 'I love you' and you say it back

I washed the office cups today, you do it tomorrow

I invite you over for dinner, then you invite me back

I drove the kids to school yesterday, it's your turn today

Gottman's research shows that the 1:1 equation is pretty much the divorce equation.

Shocking right? Considering this is what most people consider a balanced and healthy relationship it's no wonder the divorce rate is so high.

5:1 = Solid Ground: During an argument, if Gottman can observe five positive non-verbal communications such as touching, smiling, eye contact, and turning toward, to every one negative non-verbal such as eye-rolling, grimacing, sighing, and turning away, he knows this couple is on solid ground.

20:1 = Flourishing: For a marriage to really flourish Gottman maintains that the ratio is closer to 20:1. Twenty positives to every negative and this is where the magic of gratitude comes in. It is, without question, the positive interaction super-power.

Think about it. He's talking five positives during an argument!

THE SLAYING OF HORSEMEN FACTOR

You'll recall Gottman's Four Horsemen of the Apocalypse: criticism, contempt, stonewalling and defensiveness. You'll also recall how much they mess with your relationships. Gratitude is a wonderful way to slay at least two of these horsemen. Firstly, you have less to criticise and complain about when you're focusing on what you appreciate about someone. Secondly:

It's kind of hard to feel contempt while you're expressing gratitude.

THE HUMILITY FACTOR

When we begin noting the ways those around us contribute to our lives we start to see our place in the world. If it weren't for the supermarket down the road, the guy who delivers the goods to that supermarket and the farmer who grows the vegetables he delivers, we'd have to grow them on our apartment verandah.

Gratitude helps us lose the illusion that we're somehow independent of others, or somehow more special than others.

This is a wonderful side effect because it grows our ability to be more humble, a brilliant attribute to cultivate if you want better relationships.

Gratitude has increased my sense of belonging and my understanding that I'm part of something bigger. I don't survive by my efforts alone. I'm more likely to notice, appreciate and thank the delivery man, the check out chick, the lady who drives the garbage truck and all the other people who make my life easier, even possible. I'm more aware and very grateful it's not me pulling weeds on my verandah farm in an effort to feed myself. This translates to me treating the other travellers on the journey a little better.

We need each other.

THE HAPPINESS FACTOR

I've already covered how crucial happiness is to happy relationships so I'll just throw these wild and wonderful numbers into the mix and leave it at that.

Depending on what research I read, and there is plenty out there, the practice of gratitude increases overall happiness by between 22% and 25%. That is ridiculous, winning the lottery wouldn't even come close to that. Apparently this research on gratitude isn't just research with a cohort of privileged westerners.

Westerners who suddenly, during the study, realise they have hot running water and toilets. Luxuries! This research on gratitude has been carried out across many cultures. Even in cultures without toilets. It's not about what you have or do not have. Astounding.

I read that 40% of the world's population don't have toilets.

THE SEEING FACTOR

One of our greatest needs as humans, greater even than our need for love or sex, is our need to be seen. I've already mentioned this and I'm repeating it because it's so crucial to us getting on together.

By being seen I mean valued, noticed, appreciated, in short we need to know that we matter. It's the question we have our hand up asking all the time.

Abraham Maslow famously said, *'We may define therapy as a search for value.'*

When my parents were celebrating their 35th wedding anniversary my mum asked my dad if he still loved her.

His reply was both hilarious and sad. It has become the favourite of our family one-liners.

> *'I told you I loved you when we married. If anything changes I'll let you know.'*

While this line is funny I also think it is, in many ways, true of all of us. We assume people know how we feel because we once communicated it.

Or we assume we know how people feel even though we've never communicated it. I was being interviewed by the editor of a magazine after her whole team had taken part in one of my workplace workshops. I knew from being with the team that this editor was much loved by her staff. Unusually so.

When I commented on how much her team loved her, the editor was very surprised. No one in the team had actually clearly communicated their regard for her to her. It happens all the time.

If you look around at the people in your life, from family and friends to baristas and teachers, you'll likely find that most of them aren't aware of how much you value them.

When I take time to stop and really think about the many people around me and the various ways they contribute to my life, I'm overwhelmed by the richness of it all. When I express this gratitude to those people they feel seen, valued, appreciated and I give them the one thing they most want.

THE GOOD STUFF FACTOR

I'm brilliant at noticing faults in people, places and things. Take me to a five star resort and I'll be able to tell you what needs improving and who needs to change.

Again, I know, delightful traits. Still, someone has to do it.

Many years ago I had a brief brush with gratitude after a dear friend died. He was young and it was the first death in our circle of friends. I was stunned he was gone. His funeral was attended by almost 1,000 people and after chatting to them I realised I wasn't the only one who was going to miss him.

After the funeral I spent time thinking about who he was and what he'd contributed to my life. Quite a lot as it turned out. Yet the things I had most commented on, when referring to him, were his faults, which until that moment had seemed numerous. I felt, and still feel, terrible that I hadn't taken time to let him know how much he meant to me, how much he'd enriched my life.

Anxious not to make that mistake again I decided to show my appreciation to all the significant others in my life by writing long thank-you letters. The really troubling thing was realising how much easier I found it to summon up their faults than their good points. I'd quickly bring to mind the things they'd done wrong and the ways they'd let me down, and yet I had to really think about it to recall the wonderful ways they'd enriched my life.

I'd been attentive to all the wrong things!

Sadly, as with complaining, this bit of self-revelation faded quickly and it would be another 10 years before I really began to get a handle on it.

You can tell I'm a bit slow with all this stuff.

When I'm actively communicating my gratitude I'm forced to notice the good things about people, and this in turn makes me more alert to the good stuff everywhere, even in me. Gratitude helps me see what is wonderful about humanity and reduces my tendency to focus on the failings of my friends and fellow travellers.

Noticing the good in others is way more helpful for developing good relationships than focusing on their faults.

I know, I've already mentioned this. It's simple and so obvious it shouldn't have to be pointed out. However, it did have to be pointed out quite forcefully to me, so I'm very sympathetic to the fact that this is also one of those principles that is easy to miss. It bears repeating, and repeating because almost nothing in our consumer-based society points us in this direction and media encourages us to be fault-finding on a daily basis.

Stick this one on the fridge.

INTERACTIVE MINDFULNESS

The 'essentiality' of gratitude to make your relationships flourish cannot be overstated. It's seriously my biggest life tip; notice what others do for you and tell them of your gratitude.

Not for a few days, or a week, or even a month – commit to it for a year. The effect of gratitude will impact your life quite quickly yet it will be in the continued practice that you'll start to see the truly surprising transformation.

THIS IS THE PRACTICE

The practice of gratitude is the communication of appreciation.

To God, the Universe, your partner, your friends, your boss, your mother, your grandpa, your dry-cleaner, your doctor and every other person.

You'll find so much to say when you start to look for the good in your life and focus on the good in others.

AN ACT OF GRATITUDE

We're almost at the end of this book and before we part I want to end on a gorgeous story. When Phil and I were in the middle of all the pain over what had happened with these catastrophes, my eldest son gave us a healing and incredibly thoughtful gift.

He gave us a funeral.

Our darling son invited our nearest and dearest to stand up in front of us and tell us, from the bottom of their hearts, what we meant to them. People were in tears, their eulogies so real, it was as if we had actually died. The funeral was also completely hilarious because my very, funny son had asked everyone to include how and where we'd died as part of their speech. Our youngest daughter told everyone we'd died after a nude tandem parachute dive had gone wrong. One person suggested Phil had died after being crushed by his storage boxes.

Yes he's a magpie.

We saw ourselves from a new perspective. I had no idea my youngest daughter saw me as her closest friend since I had no idea she even saw me as a friend. One of my dearest friends, Pam, said she loved my nose. A nose I'd never liked. Pam wrote a poem about by my nose and my toes. Everyone also chose a song that reminded them of us. '*Talking About A Revolution*' by Tracy Chapman was one of the songs chosen for me by my kids.

I cannot imagine a more beautiful, thoughtful or meaningful gift than this funeral our dear boy gave us. It was healing. It was also an incredible way to express gratitude.

AND TO FINISH

There aren't any easy answers when dealing with humans and I found it a dilemma to decide what to include and what to leave out when writing this book. There's tons of relevant stuff I could have added but didn't because you wouldn't be able to carry the book when I was finished. Also Phil was getting lonely having a writer for a wife, he wanted me back in his life.

How ironic. Writing a book on relationships meant I had little time for any of my relationships!

Has what I've learned changed the relationships that broke down? Yes and no. Some relationships have rekindled and some haven't. As I've already said; understanding more about all this has made forgiving, accepting and all those healing practices so much easier. Of course I still have to actually practise these virtues for them to make a difference.

Sure, I'll behave like a Muggle in the future, you can count on it. However, hopefully I'll avoid some of the calamity and conflict

I've created in the past because I now behave like a Magician more frequently than I used to.

Love is a practice. Kindness is a practice. Gratitude is a practice. This is how it is with all our virtues and skills and we only improve at those skills when they're practised. Mattieu Ricard, a French Buddhist monk who works with the Dalai Lama, is reputedly the happiest man in the world had this to say:

> *'Happiness is a skill, emotional balance is a skill, compassion and altruism are skills, and like any skill they need to be developed. This is what education is all about.'*

I can work at this, I can learn to be happier, act more kindly and to love better and so can you. Doesn't this give you hope?

THE GREAT BIG BUCKET

So here we are at the end of my book about relationships. I hope you've enjoyed the journey, thank you so much for making it with me. Perhaps, if you're like me, you've made your own margin notes and dog-eared some pages that you can refer to again and again. Maybe you've already found some of the practices useful or maybe you're saving some of them up for when you need them.

If you're anything like me you'll want to know more. You'll want to read some of the books and check out the various studies I've mentioned.

To that end I've created a whole load of resources on my website and you can find a page with what you need to know at the end of this book. I've called that page '*The Great Big Bucket Page*' so that Phil has somewhere to put his bucket.

Darling, I told you we'd find somewhere for it.

On my website you'll see all the books I've mentioned and more I recommend as well as links to the research. You'll be able to read the whole story of the funeral my son organised. In a weird karmic twist my son actually got the idea for the funeral from my very cool *'Gratitude Adventure'* email program. You'll be able to find out about that adventure and also my online *'Great Full Life Class'* video course and I'll also include some cool TED talks, videos, and short films.

PRACTICE

Throw Someone A Funeral

If you really want to show someone how special they are; forget the parties and gifts. Throw funerals!

Come on, just do it. You know you want to.

LET'S BEGIN

If you've stuck with me this far we'll likely be friends forever so make sure you email and let me know what you write on this page. It's important stuff. The good life begins here when you write down the one practice that you'll start your walk to freedom with.

I'll be right here
if you need
me.

The Great Big Bucket

There's so much I'd love to share with you and to that end Phil has made a page on my website where you'll be able to find information about the following things and more.

www.tonipowell.me/greatbigbucket

THE BOOK LIST: All the great books I've mentioned in *What A Feeling!* and others I love, that I didn't have room to mention in this book, are conveniently listed for your reading pleasure.

THE HAPPINESS PAGE: There's loads of material out there in the world about getting happier. I've put some of the things I've found useful on this page.

THE RESEARCH: Some people just love a good reference. If that's you then I've included a page where you can get bogged down in all the details of the studies I mention.

RESOURCES: Anything else I think you'd like will go on the resources page. There are some TED talks, some of my blog posts, sites I like and other such delights.

WORKSHOPS/COURSES: You can find out about my workplace workshops as well as online and public events.

NEWSLETTER: I have a newsletter that I send out sporadically. You might like it because it's all about enjoying the ride.

SPEAKING: There's little I like more than telling life-changing stories so if you need such a person please email me speaker@tonipowell.me.

Acknowledgements

THANK YOU THANK YOU THANK YOU

This book is in existence because of the tireless patience and grace of Mary-Lou Stephens who was my 'book enabler'. She guided, encouraged and also did a stack of editing. Her advice was invaluable.

Mark Nebauer and my mum, Evelyn Vogt, also added so much with their incisive editing. Each of these three brought a different wisdom and each of them was key to what we, together, created in these pages. Who knew there was so much work editing a book? They did and did it anyway. Darling Phil wore his fingers to the bone laying out the book again and again because I changed my mind so often. I drew the arrows, please don't blame him.

In my book these four win the contest of generosity.

Aishah Macgill contributed wise advice, extra eyes and 'midwifed' the book to print. Patrick Walsh, our graphic designer was happily flexible and so fun to brainstorm the cover with. Jeanette Morrison was my kind copy-editor. All three of you were fast and delightful to work with.

Also Erin Hoare and Justin Robinson, at the Institute of Positive Education, were kind and generous in helping checking research.

Carol Tavris, Elliot Aronson, Maya Angelou, Dr John Medina, Dr John Gottman, Dr Dan Siegel, Shawn Achor, Michelle Gielan, W.F. Harley Jr., Mattieu Ricard, Brenè Brown, Bruce McEwan and George E. Vaillant have been just some of my teachers on this journey. Obviously I wouldn't even have had a book to write without these smart, wise people. I'm so grateful for the difference they've made to my life.

It's a treasured gift when someone you hold in high esteem is kindly toward your own work. Shawn Achor, Michelle Gielan, Justin Robinson, Petrea King, David Bott, Christine Carter, Tony Barry, and Jennifer Moss gave me such a gift when they endorsed this book.

While I included my mum's endorsement to add some fun, she did really say that and it's ended up being the endorsement that means the most to me.

And last, but definitely not least, I want to include my five children – Hailey, Isaac, Nick, Georgia and Benedicte; their partners – Andrew, Julie, Hannah and Chris; and my gorgeous grandchildren – Zali, Poppy, Abi, Baden, Zen, Milla, Priya, Theo and Florin; who are my treasured ones. They offer the most meaningful of relationships and I love them all countless Jonathans.

Jonathan Richman's music has been a source of such unfettered joy in our home that his name is now a measure of love.

About the Author

When Toni was eleven a friend of her parents asked her to see how long she could hold her breath. He just wanted her to stop asking questions for a minute. Fortunately this ploy didn't work and Toni has kept asking questions and seeking answers about the stuff that really matters like happiness, gratitude and relationships.

The discoveries she's made have transformed her from a worrywart into a gratitude maven and diminished her chronic complaining. This research has helped Toni and her husband Phil, turn their unlikely match into a marriage where a nauseating amount of hand-holding is still happening 40 years down the track.

Toni's shares all these revelations through engaging, story-based workshops, talks, books and online programs that she and her angel husband take into schools, events and workplaces.

In between hanging out in cafes, walking on the beach, watching films and trying to recall the birthdays of her five children, and nine grandchildren, Toni reads a lot of books.

www.ingramcontent.com/pod-product-compliance
Lightning Source LLC
Chambersburg PA
CBHW060314030426
42336CB00011B/1037
9780994296047